Surviving the Crash

Your Legal Rights In A Bicycle Accident

Printed in the United States of America
ISBN: 978-1-59571-947-8

Designed, printed and published:
Word Association Publishers
205 Fifth Avenue
Tarentum, Pennsylvania 15084

www.wordassociation.com

Cover photo: shutterstock.com

Surviving the Crash

Your Legal Rights In A Bicycle Accident

Bruce S. Deming, Esq.

This book is dedicated in loving memory
to my mother, Muriel Sutherland Deming.

Special thanks to my capable research assistant,
Molly Marks, for her many
contributions to the book.

"Life is like riding a bicycle.
To keep your balance you must keep moving."
Albert Einstein, letter to his son, Eduard, 1930

If the above quote resonates with you, you already know the pure joy of riding. And if you know that joy, you also know it can come at a price. Increased risk of injury is part of every cyclist's world. You know it, you accept it, and you deal with it, because in the end, the joy of riding a bike is just worth it. If it wasn't, you wouldn't ride.

"Learn to ride a bicycle. You will not regret it if you live."
Mark Twain, American author and humorist

For even the most experienced cyclist, life on the road is fragile. Despite the joy and freedom that comes from riding a bike, that freedom can be cut short in an instant by a careless driver who sends you into a bad crash.

In a blinding instant, the life you knew is changed for the worse. If you are lucky, you may end up with some minor "road rash" and bruises, and perhaps some minor bike repairs to deal with before you are back on the road.

If you're not so lucky, you could be facing serious, debilitating injuries requiring months of expensive, time consuming, and painful medical treatment, all of which will affect every part of your life: your work, your finances, and even your relationships with friends and family. Some of those injuries may have permanent consequences. If that happens, you need the best advice and legal representation you can find to make sure that your legal rights are protected, that your medical needs are met (and paid for), and that your family finances remain intact.

As a cyclist, every time you head out for a ride you are an instant target for careless motorists. No matter how careful and experienced you are, the negligent actions of another driver can happen just too fast to avoid. But if you are injured in a bad crash, you don't have to be a target twice. You don't have to be a target for smooth talking insurance adjusters who will do everything they can to avoid paying your claim, or pay you far less than you are entitled to as appropriate compensation for your serious injuries. When it comes to bicycle accidents and the law, what you don't know can hurt you. What you *do* know can save you. That is what this book is about.

Cycling is a social sport, and cyclists love to share their experiences, in person and online. We talk about gear, training techniques, nutrition, and countless other topics of interest to those of us who are passionate about the sport.

In representing cyclists who've been injured, however, I know there are a lot of "urban legends" out there about how the legal process works when it comes to bicycle accidents. Some are true, and some are not. That is why I wrote this book – to provide you, the injured cyclist, with some clear, essential information to help you make the right decisions, right away. The things you say and do in the minutes and hours after your accident can have a huge impact – positively or negatively – on the outcome of your case. You only get one shot. Make it count.

This book is not intended to be an exhaustive treatise on the law of negligence, or a "complete guide" to safe cycling. Rather, it is intended to answer the basic questions you will want answered should you find yourself injured in a crash.

Should you have more questions after reading this, I am available to help you. Contact my office any time.

Sincerely,

Bruce Deming
The Bike Lawyer

PREFACE AND DISCLAIMER

DISCLAIMER: NOTHING IN THIS BOOK SHOULD BE CONSIDERED LEGAL ADVICE, SO PLEASE DO NOT CONSIDER IT AS SUCH.

NOTHING CAN REPLACE COMPETENT ADVICE FROM A QUALIFIED ATTORNEY WHO HAS ALL THE RELEVANT FACTS ABOUT YOUR CASE, BECAUSE EVERY SITUATION IS DIFFERENT.

SINCE OUR OFFICES ARE LOCATED IN VIRGINIA, SOME OF THE INFORMATION IN HERE IS VIRGINIA-SPECIFIC, AND WHEN THAT IS THE CASE I WILL TELL YOU. OTHERWISE, THE INFORMATION PROVIDED IS GENERALLY APPLICABLE ANYWHERE IN THE U.S.

LASTLY, PLEASE REMEMBER THIS: THE OBSERVATIONS SET OUT IN THIS BOOK ARE BASED UPON MY KNOWLEDGE AND EXPERIENCE. HOWEVER, IN LAW, AS IN MOST ALL OTHER THINGS, THERE ARE EXCEPTIONS TO EVERY RULE, AND THE LAW IS CONSTANTLY EVOLVING.

CHAPTER 1

THE TYPES OF CASES WE HANDLE

My office handles bicycle, motorcycle, truck, auto, and pedestrian accidents resulting in medical injuries, primarily in Virginia, the District of Columbia, and Maryland. Because we are extremely focused on providing a high level of service to each client, **we only accept a limited number of cases a year** to ensure that our clients receive the best possible representation and outcome. Some firms will take every case that comes in the door. We approach things a little differently.

If you have been in a bicycle accident in any of these three jurisdictions, we are here to help you, and are more than pleased to speak with you. There is no obligation, and we can tell you pretty quickly whether our firm is the right firm for you, and whether your case is right for us.

We know your time is valuable, so while we are always glad to speak with you about your case, please know up front that we **do not** handle cases where:

- The client's medical bills are less than $2,000.
- The client has been convicted of (or pled guilty to) a serious moving violation as a result of the accident.

- The client is contacting us for the first time more than 18 months after the accident (Virginia cases) or more than 30 months after the accident (DC and Maryland cases).

If you are in one of these categories, please don't despair, as we can still assist. Even though your case may not be right for us, there are other great lawyers out there who may be available to help, and to whom we will gladly refer you. Give us a call and we will do what we can to help.

CHAPTER 2

RULE #1: IN THE EYES OF MANY, CYCLISTS ARE SECOND CLASS CITIZENS

Let's talk about equality, and reality. If you know anything at all about cycling and the law, then you know that cyclists generally have the same rights and responsibilities on the road as all other drivers. So cyclists should receive the same treatment by law enforcement and insurance companies as any other drivers on the road, right?

In theory, and in the eyes of the law, of course. But is that true in the real world?

Unfortunately, the answer is a resounding "no," and public perception is the reason.

The reality is this: as in all things, the actions of a few affect perceptions of the many. Every time a cyclist "rolls through" a stop light or darts recklessly in and out of traffic, the driver of that car thinks "there goes another idiot on a bicycle." Does that driver stop to think that *most* cyclists are safe, courteous, responsible citizens? Not on your life. And if that driver ends up on a jury one day – maybe on a jury deciding responsibility for a bicycle/car accident, will it impact their thinking? Of course it will.

What about police officers? Whether we're talking about local police, county police, deputy sheriffs or state troopers, the same often holds true. Despite that fact that police are trained professionals, they are also human beings subject to the same prejudices and life experience tendencies as everyone else. Every time an officer observes a cyclist doing something illegal or just plain foolish, that officer's perception of all cyclists is affected – and not for the better. Sometimes, consciously or unconsciously, that perception can adversely influence an officer's investigation of a bicycle accident.

As a result, unfortunately, the actions of a few irresponsible cyclists do affect the public's view of riders in general, and that includes highly trained, responsible police officers. How does that affect you if you are in an accident?

Significantly. Based on my personal experience, many officers are too quick to assume that a wreck involving a car and bike was caused either partly or entirely as a consequence of aggressive riding or speeding on the part of the cyclist – despite no objective evidence at the crash scene to indicate that. Quite often, there may be no objective third party eyewitnesses at the scene for the officer to interview, so the officer is left only with the statement of the rider ("Officer, he just cut in front of me!") to the statement of the driver ("That maniac was flying! He came from nowhere! I had no time to stop!").

In many cases, the officer may give the benefit of the doubt to the driver by not issuing the driver a ticket for failure to yield, improper lane change, or any other moving violation that may be supported by the evidence at the scene. When I ask officers about this, quite often they will simply say that it's the "unofficial policy of their department" to "let the lawyers figure it out," and that who was at fault for causing the accident is a "civil matter." From the perspective of the officer, taking a "neutral" stance by not issuing a citation to either party is simply that: not taking a side. From the standpoint of the insurance carrier, however, that "neutral" position is something to be used against the cyclist later on as evidence of an *absence* of negligence on the part of the driver. So rather than being a neutral party (which may be the officer's reasonable intent), the investigating officer's decision to issue no citations at all ends up favoring the driver over the bicyclist.

Is this so-called "neutral" policy fair to cyclists? No. Can it adversely affect their claim for compensation later on? Absolutely. This is because if the careless driver who caused the accident is cited for a moving violation, and ends up either pleading guilty (paying the fine is pleading guilty, by the way) or found guilty, that conviction may be evidence of negligence "per se" in the eyes of the law in a subsequent civil claim for damages.[1] In such cases, the driver's insurance carrier will be far more motivated to settle the case without proceeding to trial than they might be without such a conviction. But if no ticket is issued at all by the investigating officer, then the issue of negligence is squarely "in play," and that can have a downward pressure on any potential settlement amount to the injured cyclist who was not at fault in the accident. For more on this, see Chapter 6 on the subject of "negligence."

Does your status as a "second class citizen" end with other drivers and the police? Unfortunately, no. Insurance adjusters are on the same bandwagon, because they know that juries have the same negative pre-conceived notions of cyclist responsibility as the typical driver does. Result? Adjusters believe, often correctly, that juries are less likely to believe the version of the accident told by the cyclist than they are the "responsible" car driver. As a consequence, it influences their estimation of what a reasonable settlement value of your claim should be, thereby pushing more cases to trial and

[1] Precise definitions can and do vary by state, but Black's Law Dictionary, a frequently cited source of legal definitions, defines "Negligence Per Se" as "[C]onduct, whether of action or omission, which may be declared and treated as negligence without any argument or proof as to the particular surrounding circumstances, either because it is in violation of a statute or valid municipal ordinance, or because it is so palpably opposed to the dictates of common prudence that it can be said without hesitation or doubt that no careful person would have been guilty of it. As a general rule, the violation of a public duty, enjoined by law for the protection of person or property, so constitutes." Black's Law Dictionary, 5th Edition.

increasing the risk that the injured cyclist may receive little or no award as a consequence. Fair? No. But know this from the outset: your status as a cyclist may impact the perspective of a number of people who matter in a big way from the very moment of impact forward, regardless of your own personal driving record, and regardless of the way you ride a bike.

Are there things you can do to balance out these prejudices and misconceptions? Perhaps not entirely, because they are difficult to gauge, and of course vary on a case-by-case basis depending on who's involved. But by at least being aware of these tendencies, you now know that it is especially critical that cyclists, more than any other kind of driver on the road, *need to protect their rights to the maximum degree possible* if they are to receive a fair shake in the legal system. In this regard, bicycle cases require special expertise and experience to ensure an appropriate outcome.

CHAPTER 3

WHAT IS A "PERSONAL INJURY" CASE ANYWAY?

We have all seen distasteful advertising related to accidents, lawyers and lawsuits, most of which appears in confusing, cheesy lawyer ads on TV, roadside billboards and online. You know the ones:

"Cash for your claim!!"

"Millions recovered!!"

"We'll Fight for You!!!"

"No Recovery, No Fee!!"

"We're Tougher Than Junk Yard Dogs!!"

"We'll Fight To The Finish!!"

Many of these ads refer to the lawyers handling accident cases as "Accident Lawyers," "Car Crash Attorneys," "Truck Accident Specialists," "Negligence Attorneys," "Trial Attorneys," and lots of other variations on these phrases. But think about it. While many of these ads may grab your attention, (especially when combined with full-page graphics and photos), do they really tell you anything about the **qualifications** of these lawyers to handle ***your*** bicycle accident case?

Seldom. So let's start with the basics. Just exactly what is a "personal injury" case?

In the world of trial law, a "personal injury" claim is a broad term that applies to any kind of bicycle, motor vehicle, or pedestrian accident where someone sustained actual physical injuries as a result of someone else's carelessness, or, legally speaking, someone else's "negligence."[2] Whether the vehicles involved were bicycles, cars, tractor trailers, pickup trucks, commercial trucks, or even bicycles, if a collision caused by someone's negligence resulted in someone else getting hurt, it is a civil "personal injury" claim, and the legal principles that apply are virtually the same.

Now if someone hits your car and it's their fault, but you escaped injury, you might have a "property damage" claim, but not a "personal injury" claim because you did not incur any medical injuries. But since this book focuses on bicycles,

[2] Note here that people injured by negligent doctors generally require the services of attorneys specializing in "medical malpractice." Most often, the term "personal injury" refers to injuries resulting from vehicular accidents of some type, not medical malpractice.

we know the chances are that if you were hurt in a bad wreck involving your bike and another vehicle, you probably have a claim that includes *both* personal injury *and* property damage components.

What about the different kinds of lawyer advertising? Is there really a difference between an "accident lawyer" and a personal injury" lawyer? Generally, there is not. Most lawyers who advertise themselves as handling "personal injury " cases will handle any type of accident case, whether it involves a car, truck, or bicycle.

CHAPTER 4

WHAT IS AN ACCIDENT "CLAIM"? IS IT THE SAME AS A "CASE"?

The term "claim" is part of the language insurance adjusters and lawyers use to refer to someone's potential entitlement to compensation for their injuries due to the negligence of one or more of the drivers involved in an accident. Most of the time, the injured client's "claim" can be successfully resolved through skillful preparation and negotiating on the part of the client's lawyer with the insurance adjuster.

If, however, there are legal problems with the claim or the insurance carrier just won't be reasonable and refuses to offer a reasonable sum to adequately compensate the injured person, then the client's attorney may have to file a civil lawsuit against the negligent driver. Once the lawsuit is filed in court, the "claim" then becomes a pending "case," and the legal process formally begins. This takes place in several stages, which are described in more detail in Chapter 15. Bear in mind that all personal injury lawsuits are "civil" claims, in that they are brought by private parties alleging negligence and seeking an award of money damages. These are distinct from "criminal" cases, which are brought only by government prosecutors, and seek criminal sanctions (fines and/or jail time) for violations of the criminal code. Contrary to what some people may think, you cannot "sue" to bring criminal charges against someone, but you can sue someone in civil court for behavior that also happens to be criminal.[3]

[3] The law on this varies considerably state by state. One example would be a civil suit to recover damages from injuries inflicted through the "intentional tort" of assault and battery. Another example of a civil claim based upon behavior that may also be criminal in nature is a "wrongful death" lawsuit. Remember the civil lawsuit against O.J. Simpson for "wrongful death" that was brought by Nicole Brown Simpson's family after O.J. was acquitted in his criminal trial?

CHAPTER 5

WHO WILL PAY MY MEDICAL BILLS?

There is a lot of confusion about this. In the short run, most people will be looking to their own health insurance provider for payment of their medical bills. In certain circumstances, however, either the injured cyclist's auto or bicycle insurance policy or the other driver's insurance policy may have medical payment, or "MedPay," coverage available to help with the bills. MedPay coverage typically pays the cost of necessary medical care you receive as a result of a bicycle accident and can be used regardless of who is at fault. Often, it is limited to medical treatment received within the first three years after an accident, and is subject to a dollar cap. Also, in some jurisdictions, MedPay frequently applies only after other medical benefits are exhausted.

Unless your injuries are minor, however, MedPay coverage, if it is available, probably will not be sufficient to cover all the costs of your medical treatment.

In the longer term, if your negligence claim against the party at fault is successful, the costs of your medical treatment, including necessary future medical care, may be recoverable. The process takes time however, which is why your health insurance, when available, is essential in the short term to assure that the treatment you need is delivered in a timely fashion without legal complications.

WHAT IF I DON'T HAVE HEALTH INSURANCE?

Obviously, this is a difficult circumstance with no simple solutions. Frequently, however, hospitals and doctors may be willing to treat you without health insurance provided that you agree to sign an "assignment of claims" document that gives them a contractual "lien" (a legally enforceable right to collect first) on any settlement funds or jury awards that may result from your claims against the driver(s) at fault. At the same time, however, you will likely still be liable to those providers to some degree for payment if they don't end up receiving any such funds. I say "some degree" here because if you end up hiring an attorney, an experienced lawyer can often negotiate on your behalf with your medical providers to reduce their fees due and owing in order to work out an appropriate settlement of your claim. (Tip: Those providers know that without the lawyer's skill and hard work, they might not get paid at all, which is why they will often negotiate.)

It is important to understand, however, that once you are released from the hospital, if you have no insurance, health care providers are under no obligation to accept "assignment of claims" forms. Some will accept it and some will not, but they are under no obligation to do so.[4]

---

[4] Note: The evolution of Federal law (i.e.,"Obamacare") will likely change the landscape here in significant ways, but as of the date of this book's publication, that is the situation.

CHAPTER 6

WHAT DO I HAVE TO SHOW TO RECOVER COMPENSATION IN A CIVIL SUIT BASED ON NEGLIGENCE?

Three things. First, you have to prove "liability" on the part of the other driver by showing that he or she was legally "negligent." Second, you have to prove that the negligent act "proximately caused" your injuries and resulting economic losses ("causation"). Third, you have to prove the *extent* of your injuries and/or economic losses ("damages"). We'll discuss damages at greater length in a minute, but first let's focus on negligence and causation.

NEGLIGENCE: THE "REASONABLY PRUDENT PERSON" STANDARD

What is the definition of negligence exactly? Legally speaking, a "negligent" act is considered a "tort" or a "wrongful" act of carelessness by one individual that directly causes injury to another. More specifically, Black's Law Dictionary, often cited with authority for defining legal terms, defines "negligence" as "the failure to use such care as a reasonably prudent and careful person would use under similar circumstances…"[5]

If this sounds like a rather fluid, slippery concept, it is. What constitutes a negligent act under one set of circumstances may not be a negligent act under another. That is one reason why no two cases are ever the same, even though they may share similar attributes.

Let us consider a simple example by way of illustration. Under one scenario, a driver is driving the posted speed limit of 45 mph on a dry road on a clear, sunny day when his front tire blows out unexpectedly, causing him to lose control and veer into the oncoming lane, causing an accident. Assuming nothing he did (or didn't do) caused the tire to blow out, was

[5] This is the essence of it. If you want the more complete, formal legal definition of "negligence" from Black's, here it is:

> "The omission to do something which a reasonable man, guided by those ordinary considerations which ordinarily regulate human affairs, would do, or the doing of something which a reasonable and prudent man would not do. Negligence is the failure to use such care as a reasonably prudent and careful person would use under similar circumstances; it is the doing of some act which a person of ordinary prudence would not have done under similar circumstances or failure to do what a person of ordinary prudence would have done under similar circumstances." Black's Law Dictionary, 5th Edition (1980). (Note: This is a broad dictionary definition of the term and concept, the essence of which may vary to some degree, depending upon the particular state jurisdiction involved.)

he negligent? Maybe yes, maybe no, depending on a variety of circumstances, but he probably wasn't negligent simply for driving 45 mph if that was the posted speed limit.

Now, let us change the facts a little. Assume the driver was going the same speed on the same road (45 mph), but there was a thick, disorienting fog on the road that obscured the lane markings, causing him to veer into the oncoming lane. Was it negligent for him to be driving 45 mph in that thick fog even though he was at or just above the posted speed limit? Well, under these facts, there is certainly an argument that he was negligent because he was driving unreasonably fast considering the foggy conditions and diminished visibility. The driver's speed, when combined with the different road conditions, may result in the court applying a different standard of care against which the reasonableness of his actions are to be judged by the court and jury if the case goes to trial. In other words, what may be "negligent" under one set of conditions may not be under another.

Let's examine another example that is common to cycling accidents. A cyclist is riding his bike on a sidewalk fairly fast (say 15-20 mph), when a car exiting a parking garage driveway broadsides him and causes serious injuries. The law of that jurisdiction says it is legal to ride a bike on a sidewalk. The driver was obligated to keep a look out and yield to traffic when existing a driveway. Who was at fault, legally speaking?

Well, one can argue that the motorist was negligent for failing to yield the right of way, and they would be right. But the analysis doesn't stop there. Even though it was legal, the cyclist's decision to ride at that speed on a sidewalk may open him up to an argument that he was negligent as well, given the circumstances of where he was riding. If it is determined that the cyclist's negligence also contributed to the accident, then depending on the jurisdiction, the cyclist's "contributory negligence" could bar him from recovery. That is the law in 5 states, including DC, Maryland and the Commonwealth of Virginia, and is often a very significant factor in bicycle cases.[6]

These brief examples illustrate why you should never rely upon the advice of your fellow cyclists or well-meaning family members, who are more than eager to give you their "legal advice" based upon what happened in their case that was "just like yours." Remember this: <u>no</u> case is "just like yours," no matter how similar it may appear. That's why getting competent legal advice based upon a thorough understanding of your particular case, with all of its factual and legal subtleties, is the only way to properly determine the merits and value of your claim.

[6] It is also the law currently in North Carolina and Alabama. For more information on the important doctrine of contributory negligence, see Chapter 13.

DAMAGES: WHAT ARE THEY? HOW MUCH AM I ENTITLED TO RECOVER?

If you are injured in an accident caused by the negligence of another driver, what types of compensation are you entitled to recover?

As we mentioned, compensation for injuries sustained in an accident is referred to as one's "damages," and in most jurisdictions, include

- your reasonable and necessary medical expenses and costs of treatment and therapy for injuries sustained;
- lost wages for time away from work due to hospitalization, medical treatment and recovery;
- future reasonable and necessary medical expenses;
- property damages (the physical damage to your bicycle and riding accessories), and
- last but not least - compensatory damages for the "pain and suffering" incurred by you as a result of your injuries.

In addition to these types of damages, in very rare cases, and I mean VERY rare, "punitive damages" can be awarded -- not to compensate you, the plaintiff, but to actually *punish* the defendant for negligent actions so extreme and reckless that they deserve it.[7] Contrary to the "tort reform" ads you may have heard produced by the insurance industry, however, these types of damages are not favored under the law of Virginia or the District of Columbia, and are rarely awarded. And although emotionally you may want to "punish" that negligent driver for the injuries they caused you, it is important to remember that the primary function of a civil claim for negligence is to *compensate* you for injuries sustained, *not punish* the other guy. Punishment for wrongdoing is the primary function of the criminal courts, not the civil.

PRE-EXISTING INJURIES

Things also get interesting here, so by way of example, let's assume the following facts surrounding a common scenario I see in my practice quite often. Say you herniated (i.e.,"slipped") a disc in your lower back four or five years ago, and after a lot of physical therapy and treatment, the pain has finally subsided to where it generally doesn't bother you anymore. Then one fine Saturday morning when you are out

[7] This is true in Virginia and DC, but varies considerably on a state-by-state basis. If you are injured in another jurisdiction, consult with a local attorney who can advise you on the burden of proof required to establish punitive damages in your state. The requirements vary widely.

for a ride with your friends on Skyline Drive[8], a careless driver enjoying too long a look at the Shenandoah Valley veers into your lane and runs you off the road. Your bike is a little banged up, but fortunately you have only a few bruises and scrapes - no broken bones or serious injuries as far as you can tell. Over the next few days, however, that old back injury flares up with a vengeance.

Not being a whiner, you tough it out with Advil for a few days hoping it will go away. But it doesn't. Then, by the end of the week, you're in such pain you can hardly get out of bed, and finally go to your orthopedist, who confirms what you already know. You have "re-injured" that nagging disc in your back. Have you suffered compensable damages from the recent accident even though it is related to a pre-existing injury?

The quick answer is *yes,* but the challenge is proving it. In this case you have to prove that *this* particular driver's negligence caused *these* re-injuries. If they are substantial, the insurance adjuster (or the insurance company's lawyer if a lawsuit has to be filed) will want to go through all of your prior medical

[8] For those of you not familiar with rural Virginia, Skyline Drive is a particularly spectacular and scenic ride along a beautiful ridge through the Shenandoah National Park. The views are awesome, but the twists and turns can leave cyclists vulnerable to careless motorists gawking at the scenery.

records to determine the precise nature of your pre-existing injury, and look carefully at all of your doctors' notes from each and every one of your prior treatments. Why? Well, the insurance company wants to determine that your old injury really had resolved *prior* to the accident. If you had seen your doctor for the old injury as recently as a few months or even weeks before the accident, the insurance adjuster is going to discount the value of your claim (or even deny it entirely) because your back was already hurting anyway, and your fairly recent visit to the doctor proves it.

That's wrinkle number one. Another wrinkle is that your delay in getting medical treatment may be a "red flag" to the adjuster that you are exaggerating your injury. This is a point that bears strong emphasis. If you delay in getting medical attention for your injuries for days or weeks after the accident, that delay lends further support to the insurance company's position that this "new" injury is not as bad as you say it is, and may be entirely unrelated to your recent accident.

What is the lesson here? If you have even the slightest feeling that a crash may have resulted in injuries to you, **get checked out without delay.** If things resolve quickly, then good for you. But if they don't, and do actually worsen in the coming days, at least you will have a record of having documented your injury in a timely manner by seeking prompt medical attention immediately following the accident.

To review: from a legal standpoint, injured people *are* entitled to recover for preexisting injuries made worse by the carelessness of another. But proving up the incremental damage caused by the defendant's negligence is made more complicated and difficult by the existence of a plaintiff's pre-existing injury, and this complexity can substantially reduce the value of your claim, particularly if there is a delay between the date of the accident and the date that you first seek medical attention. A good lawyer will ask you detailed questions about your pre-existing injuries and treatment history, and will ask you to sign a release so that he or she can obtain your medical records and review them carefully. By understanding the details of your medical history and treatment, your lawyer will be well armed to negotiate effectively with the insurance adjuster, and if necessary, to take your case to trial if the circumstances require it.

CHAPTER 7

WHAT TO DO (AND NOT DO) RIGHT AWAY IF YOU'VE BEEN IN A BICYCLE ACCIDENT

- Stay put, and get immediate medical attention. If you've gone down hard, don't make a move until help arrives. Feeling numbness in any of your extremities? If you've injured your spine or sustained internal injuries, any significant movement could put you at serious risk. Await professional help whenever you can do so safely.
- If witnesses can be identified, ask them to give you their names and numbers **right away**. If you are in no condition to collect that information, ask someone to do it for you, and don't be shy about it. Most smartphones have a "notes" feature that can be used to record such information – use it. You'd be amazed at how fast caring witnesses can appear, and then quickly fade into the woodwork and drift away once they see that medical attention and/or the police have arrived and that you are being taken care of. I believe in the goodness of my fellow humans, but in the end, lots of people who will eagerly tell you they "saw everything" often decide within a few minutes that they just don't want to get involved. Get their names and numbers RIGHT AWAY so that they can be found again if their testimony is needed. If you've been hurt, it will be.

- If you or other witnesses on the scene have a cellphone camera or even regular camera, use it! Take pictures of the scene, the vehicles involved, your bike, and you. Take as many as you can. Too many is not enough. I've handled many cases where one single photograph, taken at the scene or later at the hospital, made all the difference later on in establishing liability – an essential element of an injured person's claim for compensation. Once the vehicles are moved and the scene is cleaned up, you've lost an important opportunity to document what happened. If you can't do it, ask someone else to, and be sure to get their contact info so they can email you the pictures. Again, don't be shy about this. Your rights may depend on it, and once the opportunity is gone, well, it's gone.
- Once medical help arrives, if you find yourself in a hospital emergency room, cooperate fully with your doctors and attending nurses, but don't volunteer a lot of detail about how the accident happened unless they specifically ask you for purposes of understanding your injuries.[9] Quite often, accident victims are in shock and details can be hazy – especially if you're on an IV with strong painkillers. If you give confusing information and someone writes it down wrong in your chart, those statements can come back to haunt you later if they differ from more accurate, subsequent

[9] Please use your common sense here. Obviously, if a doctor is asking you a specific question about the impact or anything else that bears upon treatment, I'm not suggesting for one second that you hold back information that could be vitally important to your proper diagnosis and treatment.

statements and accounts rendered later on. Even if you are clear headed when you arrive at the hospital, I've seen cases where ER personnel simply misunderstood a patient's description of the accident and put the wrong information down on the chart.

- Here's a common example: "Patient sustained injuries after falling off his bike." This suggests that the crash was a result of poor bike handling, and neglects to mention that the cyclist "fell off his bike" because he was struck by a motorist at high speed.
- Avoid these issues by simply answering their questions and staying focused on your care and treatment. If you insist on telling anyone and everyone in that ER what happened over and over (as many people want to do when they've just been through a traumatic event such as a bicycle wreck), the chances are someone is going to write it down on your chart in a way that is inaccurate, incomplete, or both. That is not helpful.
- If you are transported to a hospital, call a friend or loved one immediately. Have them take photos of you and your injuries at the hospital or as soon as possible in the days thereafter (at an appropriate time, of course, so you don't interfere with treatment and of course respect the privacy of other patients). It can be valuable in thoroughly documenting the nature and extent of your injuries sustained. Don't be embarrassed to do it. No one else will.
- Follow up with all recommended medical treatment in the weeks and months following the accident. *I cannot emphasize this enough.* Unexplained "gaps" in treatment may have a significant, adverse effect upon your case.

- If another vehicle caused your accident and took off in a "hit and run," make sure you file an *immediate report* with the local police. If you are physically unable to go to the appropriate police station to file a report, call the police to report it – that day - from the hospital if necessary. If you have uninsured motorist insurance coverage, your policy may cover your injuries regardless, but if you fail to file a timely police report, the odds are that your carrier will deny the claim. If that happens you may have to file a "John Doe" suit against your own insurance carrier to secure your recovery – an uncertain recovery that could take much longer than might otherwise be necessary had the incident been reported to the authorities in a timely manner.

- Don't give statements to insurance adjusters - especially adjusters representing the other driver's insurance company - unless you have at least spoken with an attorney. Typically, you will receive a phone call from an adjuster within a day or two – sometimes even within hours – of the accident. I've seen clients who were called at the hospital, while they were heavily medicated for pain. These people will come across as the most caring, compassionate friend you've ever had. They just want to "ask you a few questions for the file" so they can "take care of everything for you," etc., etc. Typically, once they establish rapport with you, they will ask "if it's okay to record a short statement" from you just to "complete the file." **DON'T DO IT.** They also may ask you to sign and fax over "a few simple forms" to begin the claims process and "make sure you are taken care of right away." **DON'T DO IT.**

- I am not trying to make a blanket statement about all adjusters here because I have worked with a great many who were ethical, honest and straightforward. I have also worked with a great many who were none of these things, and who will do or say anything to get you to compromise your case. In some cases, adjusters may try to get answers to questions completely out of context, so they can use them later to make a case for contributory negligence, thereby making it potentially impossible for you to be compensated. So don't fall victim to these practices. Tell them you will be in touch with them in a few days, get their name and phone number, and politely hang up. The longer you stay on that phone (and believe me, they will say anything to try and keep you on that phone), the greater the risk that you will say something that could jeopardize your claim.

- If and when a statement is made to an adjuster to the effect that no physical contact was made between your bike and the offending vehicle, rest assured that they will deny the claim. Are you entirely certain there was no contact? Be careful what you say if you are not.

- Say little or nothing about how the accident happened to anyone unless asked directly by an officer, before and after you leave the accident scene (see Chapter 13, Contributory Negligence). For example, despite their excellent training, plenty of officers unfortunately have an attitude toward bicycles and speed and may try to get you to admit you were speeding without any objective evidence that you were doing so. There is nothing to be gained and everything to lose by trying to estimate your actual speed at the time of the crash after the fact. Don't do it. Be aware that any admission at all on your part could spell the end of your claim due to the doctrine of contributory negligence if it applies in your jurisdiction.

- Keep a personal journal of your treatments, including related time away from work. (Note all doctor visits and dates, and treatment received.) If you have a laptop or tablet computer, or even a little notebook, use it to add a few sentences a day to record what is going on with your injuries, your symptoms, your treatment, and your life as it has been affected by the accident. You would be amazed at how quickly you can lose track of dates and specific types of treatment you received. Keeping track of it all may be tedious, but it will be enormously helpful to your case down the road, and a great help to your attorney should you decide to hire one.

- Also use your journal to carefully track time off from work for injury-related medical treatments, and document your reason for taking leave with your employer, including time taken for travel to and from subsequent doctor's and physical therapy appointments if you have them. (Lost wages need to be thoroughly documented with pay stubs and written statements from employers confirming that you were absent and why.)

CHAPTER 8

DO I REALLY NEED A LAWYER?

Not necessarily. In many cases, your injuries from a bike accident may be limited, your medical bills low, and your property damage small as well. Generally speaking, it may not be necessary to retain a lawyer under these circumstances, because the legal fees alone could eat up most of the settlement funds, leaving very little left over for you, the injured person. But you would be well advised to at least talk to an attorney before making that decision. Even if your medical expenses and property damages are low, many qualified personal injury lawyers will make themselves available for a reasonable consulting fee to help you settle the case yourself if you decide that's best for you. Depending on the facts of your case, this might be a good option for you, and could save you $$ thousands.

On the other hand, if your injuries and / or property damages are more substantial, without question you should discuss your case with a qualified attorney to help you determine if legal representation is appropriate. And you don't have to take my word for it. Insurance industry studies confirm that insurance company payouts in cases where injured persons are represented by an attorney are substantially higher than those that are not.[10]

"BUT MY CASE IS A "SLAM DUNK!" THE OTHER GUY WAS AT FAULT! THERE'S NO WAY THE INSURANCE COMPANY ISN'T GOING TO PAY UP! WHY WOULD I NEED TO PAY A LAWYER?

Unfortunately, what may appear to be a "slam dunk" to someone who is not an attorney trained in negligence law often is not, so be forewarned. If your case involves serious injuries, at least discuss it with a qualified attorney and keep an open mind. It may not be as strong a case as you think, and having competent, experienced representation might make all the difference in your case. (For more on this, see Chapter 13 on "contributory negligence.")

---

[10] If you are interested, one excellent source of information on this is the Insurance Research Counsel that publishes studies on insurance claims and costs. You can see summaries of their available reports at http://www.insurance-research.org

CHAPTER 9

LEGAL FEES – CAN I AFFORD A LAWYER? HOW DOES MY LAWYER GET PAID?

- Most personal injury lawyers will agree to represent you on a "contingent fee" basis. What this means is that the lawyer will only get paid out of the proceeds from any cash settlement or jury award that is collected in your case. The actual percentage is often negotiable, though it is generally in the range of 33%. Some lawyers, however, insist upon a contingent fee of 40% or higher *if* the case has to proceed to litigation or an actual full trial. Experienced lawyers will tell you this is often justified because preparing for, and actually trying your case to a jury takes a substantial amount of time, and therefore increased risk to both you and the lawyer. If the jury awards nothing, then you walk away with nothing, and the lawyer doesn't get paid. As a consequence, the lawyer views trial as "higher risk . . . higher reward," and therefore may want you to agree to a higher percentage if a settlement or jury award is recovered. This is a common practice, and in my opinion there is nothing wrong with it, as long as the percentages are reasonable.
- Please be mindful that not all lawyers offer contingent fees, and those that do won't necessarily insist on the percentages referenced above. But these are common percentages

applicable to contingent fees throughout the United States, so don't be surprised if the fee agreement your potential lawyer asks you to sign includes fees at these levels.

WHAT IS THE DIFFERENCE BETWEEN A "COST" AND A "FEE?" ARE THEY THE SAME THING?

No they are not, and the difference is important for you to understand. Whenever you discuss "fees" and "costs" with your lawyer, you should know that the "contingent fee" does not include out of pocket "costs" incurred for prosecuting your claim. Typically, these costs include:

- out of pocket expenses paid by the lawyer for court filing fees (if a lawsuit has to be filed);
- deposition transcript fees (the fees charged by court stenographers to take down what people say at their depositions);
- copying charges;
- fees charged by doctor offices and hospitals for producing medical records and bills;
- doctors fees for providing expert testimony at trial (if necessary) and a number of other things.
- expert witness fees where applicable
- travel expenses where applicable

It is always a good idea to discuss these charges with your lawyer in advance and find out what they are estimated to be in your case, and when you will be expected to pay them. Quite often, your lawyer may ask you for an initial deposit of money to be placed in a "trust account" for payment of some of these out-of-pocket costs before any work is begun. The amount is normally negotiable.

In a simple accident case involving one or two witnesses, your "costs" may easily run into hundreds of dollars depending on the severity of your injuries and the complexity of your case. In more complex cases involving a lot of witnesses, doctor testimony, expert witness testimony, physician depositions and travel time, costs can run into tens of thousands of dollars. Be sure to discuss these with your lawyer, as they are NOT part of the "contingent fee" arrangement, and you will likely be responsible for paying them regardless of the outcome of your case.

You mean my doctor is going to *charge me thousands of dollars* to testify in court about my injuries and treatment? In most cases, yes. Not only will your doctor charge you anywhere from a few thousand to ten thousand dollars (and up) to testify, but he or she often will do anything possible to avoid having to do it. Doctors generally dislike having to testify in court, because it takes valuable time away from their busy (and lucrative) practices, so they charge accordingly.

I have the highest respect for treating physicians, and have no problem with them for charging appropriate fees for their time. But it is important for you as the client to be aware of these significant potential costs should you and your lawyer decide that a case should go to trial. There is no "money back guarantee" that their testimony will produce a winning verdict, and they will expect to be paid regardless – almost always in advance.

TIP: If your lawyer tells you that your doctor wants $10,000 to testify at trial, ask him if the same doctor will agree to a "de bene esse" (pronounced: "day bennay essay") videotaped deposition. This is where a physician will agree to have his testimony videotaped at a specifically scheduled time at the end of his or her workday. Physicians who agree to this type of testimony will charge you substantially less – often a *lot* less - than they would for live testimony, because they don't have to wait around the courthouse all day waiting to testify. While the effectiveness of video testimony at trial may be a little less than live witness testimony, it can still be powerful and credible if handled appropriately.

CHAPTER 10

HIRING AN ATTORNEY—HOW TO DO IT RIGHT

Okay, so you've been injured in a bicycle accident, and you feel it is the other driver's fault. You're just home from the hospital, and you are starting to get calls from the other driver's insurance adjuster. Like most people who have never been injured in an accident before, it may be that you've never had the need to hire an attorney for anything, much less something as important as handling your accident claim properly. Unless you have an existing relationship with a good lawyer who can either represent you or refer you to a qualified lawyer who can, the process of hiring one can be confusing and frustrating. How should you go about it? Here are a few suggestions.

WHAT KIND OF LAWYER DO I NEED? THERE ARE SO MANY DIFFERENT KINDS. WHICH KIND IS BEST FOR MY CASE?

You need a lawyer who is well versed in representing plaintiffs in personal injury cases. Many firms practice what is called "insurance defense" law, meaning that they only represent insurance companies against people who have been injured. You are looking for the lawyer on the other side – the lawyers who represents the claimant (otherwise known as the "plaintiff") if and when a lawsuit is filed.

WHERE DO I LOOK FOR ONE?

If you have a good existing relationship with a family lawyer, you may wish to start there. If your lawyer doesn't practice in this area, he or she may know several well qualified lawyers in your area to whom they can refer you. If they value their relationship with you, they will likely steer you to someone you can trust to handle your case properly.

If you've been in a bike accident, ask for a referral from other fellow cyclists – either training partners, teammates, or club members if you belong to one. Bicycle accidents resulting in compensable injuries are part of the cycling landscape, and the chances are that some cyclist you know has probably already been through the experience, and can provide a good recommendation. The vast majority of my cases originate with referrals from friends or family members of other cyclists I have represented in the past. If your cycling club or team uses an email "list serve" on the web, that is a good place to start.

An excellent source of helpful information can be your local bicycle advocacy group. Here in the Washington, DC, metropolitan area, the Washington Area Bicyclist Association (www.WABA.org) offers helpful guidance to injured cyclists on a number of topics, including competent lawyers who specialize in bike accident cases. Similar cycling organizations in other areas offer the same service.

Another approach is to call your local county bar association, or to check out some of the more prominent attorney listing sites on the web, such as www.lawyers.com or www.findlaw.com. Bear in mind, though, that in the case of the local bar association, the only criteria for being listed in the referral service is to be a dues paying member. Similarly, the only criteria for being listed on the big attorney search websites is to pay their subscription fees. That doesn't mean that good lawyers can't be found on these sites, but it does mean that you shouldn't put much stock solely in the fact that attorneys are listed there.

Of course, you can always use Google to search for personal injury or bicycle accident lawyers in your town or county. Once you've identified a few lawyers who have a strong presence on the web, take a good look at their sites to get a feel for what they have to tell you. If their sites contain helpful information you can use about personal injury law, the process, and their approach to representing their clients, that is a good sign, and you can use that information to make a decision about whether to schedule a meeting with them.

On the other hand, may attorney websites are simply online versions of the cheesy full page ads that we talked about earlier, wth big color photos of bad car crashes, trumpeting "millions recovered," etc. If the site does nothing but tell you how great the lawyer is, or how much money they have recovered, that is not a good sign. That's because, in my opinion, the lawyers who have the strongest credentials usually don't have to focus so much on trumpeting their accomplishments because they already have more business than they can (or want) to handle. Typically, those lawyers are more interested in informing and helping their potential clients make sound choices and prudent decisions about how to pursue their claims.

WHEN SHOULD I HIRE ONE?

Depending on the circumstances of your case, you may not need to hire a lawyer at all. As we said above in Chapter 8, if your medical bills and property damages are relatively low, you may be better off either trying to settle the matter yourself, or paying a reasonable consulting fee to an attorney for some helpful advice to guide you through the process.

If your bills and damages are more substantial, however (and if you've been in a bad bicycle wreck the chances are strong that they are), you are well advised to at least meet with a few attorneys *as soon as possible* after the accident. Earlier is definitely better, so that you don't end up making serious mistakes that could damage or even crater your claim. You also will want to preserve meaningful evidence and obtain witness statements as soon as possible so that they are both available and reliable should you need them to support your claim down the road.

Okay, I've located a few firms that look promising through recommendations from former clients or through careful use of the web. What do I do next?

Well, call them up, and ask for an appointment so that you may come in to discuss your case. Many, if not most, attorneys handling personal injury accident cases will not charge you for this "initial consultation," but you should ask up front when you call to be sure. Reputable lawyers should welcome the opportunity to speak with you in a relaxed, professional manner. Draw up a list of questions that you want to ask, and take notes. After you have spoken with a few lawyers, the chances are you will have a pretty good idea of which firm – and attorney – is the right one to handle your case.

Who you hire is, of course, ultimately a personal decision based upon your own diligent research and your basic, gut-level impression of the lawyers you speak with. To assist you, I've put together some thoughts and suggestions on the "dos" and "don'ts" of hiring a personal injury attorney, and some important questions that you may wish to ask.

CHAPTER 11

LAWYERS TO AVOID

Lawyers who pressure you to hire them immediately.

It is a sign that they are chasing you for business, and if they are desperate for new cases, there is usually a reason.

"We handle everything" law firms.

If a firm's ads indicate that they handle corporate, tax, real estate, bankruptcy, estate planning, criminal law, environmental law, patent law, and, uh, … oh by the way, **accidents**, etc., etc., you may want to be more selective. In my opinion, lawyers are no different than other trained professionals in this critical respect: the more they focus on one or two areas of expertise, the more competent and experienced they are likely to be in that area of practice.

Lawyers who are not really familiar with cycling and what it takes to prove a bicycle negligence case.

Many personal injury lawyers will actually shy away from bicycle accident cases because they are all too familiar with Rule #1 – cyclists are often disrespected by adjusters, police officers and juries due to unfortunate but common preconceptions. What you *want* is a lawyer who *understands* these prejudices and how to deal effectively with them – a lawyer who actually *likes* representing injured cyclists, and who will work hard to overcome those prejudices and get you the successful result you expect and deserve. These lawyers do exist, and they are the ones to look for.

Lawyers who take more cases than they can handle (and make their money on volume rather than securing great results for each client).

I know of a personal injury "mill" firm in the Washington, DC, area that attracts unsuspecting clients by charging an extremely low contingent fee of 25% instead of the usual 33 – 40%. Using this approach, they make a ton of money. How? Well, they pull a lot of clients in the door by offering the lower contingent fee percentage. Then, once they sign up a client, they accept the very first low-ball settlement offer that comes from the insurance adjuster. If the client balks at accepting it, the firm "sells" that offer to the unsuspecting client by telling him that his case has some "problems" and that he'd better take the low-ball settlement because going to trial is "just too risky." By employing this strategy countless times a year, these accident case mills "churn" a high annual caseload resulting in big profits for the firm but poor often results for the clients. I consider this practice to be shameful, but unfortunately, to varying degrees, it is all too prevalent.

Questions to ask:

Approximately how many pending personal injury cases is the firm handling at this time? If the lawyer proudly announces "thousands" or even "hundreds," and it's just the one lawyer and a few paralegals in the office, perhaps you should consider speaking with another lawyer with a more manageable caseload who is willing to devote the time necessary to handle your case properly.

Lawyers that make promises they can't deliver ("millions recovered!!")

Questions to ask:

- If every case is different, what does your past success have to do with my case?
- How long have you been in practice?
- What do these past recoveries have to do with my case if every case is unique?
- Have you "recovered millions" because you run a high volume mill or because you've taken some hard-to-prove cases to trial and won substantial verdicts?

Unlike many large personal injury firms, I do not publish specific dollar amounts when describing "case results" for the simple reason that such numbers can be inherently misleading. Amounts recovered in the past have nothing to do with potential recoveries in the future. Reasonable minds can differ on this subject, and there are plenty of lawyers who will disagree with me, but my philosophy is that it is not a good practice and does not contribute to sound legal information being disseminated to the public. In my view, it is misleading to the potential client.

These are tough questions, and they should be, so don't feel like you are unfairly putting that lawyer on the spot. Some of the answers you get may make sense to you, and some may not. You will be the judge.

Indulge me a moment to tell you a quick story. At his request, I once visited a potential client in the hospital, just a few days after a devastating bicycle accident. He was an experienced, safe rider who was going under the posted speed limit. A pickup at an intersection going the other way had turned left in front of him, causing him to hit the bed of the truck at 30 mph. His pelvis was crushed, his knee badly damaged, and his lung collapsed at the scene. If it hadn't been for a fast helicopter evacuation and an expert trauma and surgical team, he surely would have lost his life.

After I had obtained some initial information about the crash, I asked him if he had questions about my background and approach to bike cases. His very first question was this: "What percentage of your trials have you won and what percentage have you lost?"

My answer to his question went something like this. "I don't know, because I don't keep those numbers. When he shot me a skeptical look, I told him the following. "If by 'winning,' you are talking about a jury award after a full trial on the merits, I can tell you that I've won some cases and lost some cases. That is true of any capable trial attorney, because regardless of the evidence, juries are unpredictable, and no matter how effective you are in the courtroom, you never know how they are going to assess a given set of facts or circumstances, or how they are going to weigh your entitlement to compensation."

I further explained the following. "Look at it this way. What if I told you that I had won 99% of my cases? Would that mean that I'm the best trial lawyer in Virginia, or would it mean that I'm a lazy, mediocre lawyer that only takes easy cases to trial and settles all the tougher cases for pennies on the dollar without a fight?

He paused and smiled. "That's a fair answer, counselor." He called to hire me the next day.

I tell you this story to make a point about sizing up the attorney candidates who may be interested in representing you. There's no magic to it, friends. Listen to the answers the lawyer gives you, and trust your instincts and good common sense. If the attorney is trying to "sell" you a little too hard on his or her abilities based on information that isn't really relevant to *you* and *your case*, there may be a reason.

Lawyers who treat your case like a "file to be processed" rather than a claim to be resolved.

Question to ask:

Who will be my primary point of contact once work on my case begins: you the lawyer or a designated associate attorney, paralegal or secretary?

This is a tough one to gauge, so let me start by saying there is nothing wrong with a lawyer who makes effective use of associates, law clerks and paralegals in his or her practice. This is because all accident claims, including bicycle accident claims, are paper intensive. There are countless letters to be written, medical records and bills to be obtained and reviewed, and insurance documents to review. In the right context, trained legal professionals other than attorneys are perfectly well qualified to do this essential "legwork" so that the lawyer's time on the case is spent most efficiently and most effectively. There is nothing wrong with that.

At the same time, some firms – okay, a *lot* of firms in my opinion -- carry this principle way too far. When that happens, the lawyer loses contact with the file completely, and in the worst cases, loses contact with the client completely. The client places call after call to the lawyer for weeks or months after the initial retainer agreement is signed, and try as they might, can never seem to receive a call back from anyone other than a secretary or other staff member. This is a terrible practice, causes frustration and anger on the part of the client, and damages the most important part of the attorney-client relationship: trust and confidence. It is no wonder that countless surveys have shown "failure to timely return phone calls" as the number one complaint that clients have about lawyers.

By asking the lawyer who the primary point of contact will be, and most importantly, how clerks and paralegals are used in the firm, you will get a sense of that lawyer's philosophy about how cases, and more importantly, how clients, are handled. The same adage applies again here, friends: listen to the answers the attorney gives you, and trust your instincts.

Lawyers who chase you for business ("runners" at the hospital – unethical but common practice).

Did the lawyer insist on sending someone to the hospital to get you to sign a retainer agreement within minutes or a few hours of speaking with you on the phone? Or even worse, did someone (like an EMT) or any other non-lawyer approach you at the hospital (or even in the ambulance) offering to contact a "great lawyer" for you?

This is an age old practice of a lawyer using "runners" to solicit (i.e., run after) business from injured people before they have a chance to seek legal representation elsewhere. These "runners" are often paid by the lawyer (sometimes out of a percentage of the earned fee) to bring in new clients. It is unethical misconduct at its worst, but it still goes on just about everywhere – especially in large urban areas.

This is an easy one. No caveats, no exceptions. Run away. Lawyers who use "runners" are unethical, and deserve to be sanctioned for their misconduct. I cannot say it any plainer than that.

Lawyers who pressure you to sign a "contingent fee" retainer agreement without giving you time to thoroughly read and understand it.

Questions to ask:

Has the attorney you have spoken with encouraged you to take your time to review the agreement and answered all of your questions thoroughly and carefully? Are you entirely comfortable that you understand all aspects of the agreement? Is it written plainly and clearly?

If the answer to all of these questions is "yes," then wonderful. Any reputable lawyer will do just that. On the other hand, if the lawyer seems in a big rush to get your signature on an agreement so he or she can "start work right away" without making sure you are doing so with a complete understanding of the agreement, that lawyer is chasing you for business, and it's time to speak with another attorney. Pardon me, but this bears repeating. If that lawyer has to chase clients for business, rest assured there's a reason for it.

Lawyers who tell you they'll have your case settled "in no time" and will put "money in your pocket" quickly.

Question to ask:

When can I expect negotiations to begin with the insurance company? Can I get a check quickly?

If the lawyer's answer is "as soon as possible!" it's probably time to speak with another lawyer. An experienced lawyer knows that if you have been injured in an accident, it is important that you receive thorough and timely medical care for your injuries, and that you reach what is generally referred to as "maximum medical improvement" (otherwise known as "MMI") before making a formal demand for settlement in your case. Otherwise, if your attorney pushes you to settle the case prematurely and your injuries result in unforeseen complications or simply take a turn for the worse during treatment, your case will have been undervalued at the time of settlement and it will be too late to reopen the claim. Except in very rare cases involving fraud, once the insurance check is issued and you sign a release, that's the end of it. There are no "do overs" when it comes to settlement.

CHAPTER 12

LAWYERS TO HIRE

- Lawyers who are experienced with bicycles and bicycle accident cases
- Lawyers who ride themselves, and can understand the nuances of motorist / bicycle interaction because they live it every day
- Lawyers who do not accept every case that walks in the door, and are careful to maintain manageable caseloads so that they can give each case the attention it deserves
- Lawyers that don't need to hire "runners" to chase you for business
- Lawyers who have handled bicycle claims for friends and family, if possible, and who come highly recommended based upon personal experience
- Lawyers who will insist that you review their fee agreements carefully before signing them
- Lawyers who will meet with you, answer ALL of your questions, and who take the time necessary to ensure that your case is right for them and they are right for you

- Lawyers who are interested in educating you about bicycle claims and what you can expect so that you can make a sound decision, rather than simply just trumpeting their own past accomplishments.

CHAPTER 13

CONTRIBUTORY NEGLIGENCE!

(IF IT SOUNDS SCARY, IT IS. AND IF YOU READ NOTHING ELSE IN THIS BOOK, READ THIS!!)

Historically, the doctrine of "contributory negligence" referred to a rule where, if the injured party was guilty of negligence, no matter how slight (and I'm talking 1% here), that person was **barred from recovery** from the other negligent party who was 99% negligent and responsible for causing his injuries.[11] Over time, however, most states modified this harsh rule in favor of the doctrine of "comparative negligence," where the injured party could still recover, but would have the amount reduced by the comparative amount of his own negligence.

Today, however, Virginia is one of a handful of states (including Maryland, the District of Columbia, North Carolina and Alabama) where **the harsh doctrine of contributory negli-**

[11] Black's Law Dictionary, 5th Edition, defines "Contributory Negligence" as "The act or omission amounting to want of ordinary care on [the]part of [the]complaining party, which, concurring with defendant's negligence, is [the] proximate cause of injury. [cite omitted] Conduct by a plaintiff who is below the standard to which he is legally required to conform for his own protection and which is a contributing cause which cooperates with the negligence of the defendant in causing the plaintiff's harm."

gence still applies. If your accident occurs in one of these jurisdictions, you need to be keenly aware of it.

To review: If the other guy who caused your accident was 99% responsible, and you were 1% responsible, you are barred from recovering a single penny, no matter how serious your injuries are.

Let's look at a brief example. You're riding your bicycle down the road and a car going the other direction makes a left hand turn right in front of you. You collide with the side of the car, and incur life threatening injuries. Clearly, the other driver was negligent for any number of reasons, the most of significant of which is probably failure to yield the right of way. Negligence on the part of that driver is clearly established.

Now, in the hospital, the officer comes to visit you, and asks you how fast you were going at the time of the accident in order to complete his accident report. Through the haze of painkillers, you say "I'm not sure – around 35-40 mph I guess." Later on, it turns out that the post speed limit was 30 mph. Guess what? You may have just admitted to speeding at the time of the accident, which is possibly "negligence per se" and therefore a legitimate basis for the other guy's insurance carrier to cry "contributory negligence." If the case goes to trial, you risk walking away with zero as a result, even though the other driver was legally negligent.

There is an important aspect to this that bears emphasis hoever. Even if the cyclist is found to have been negligent in some way, the negligent act must have *actually contributed* to the cause of the accident. For example, I represented a badly injured cyclist a few years back who was broadsided by an SUV emerging from a parking lot. The accident occurred after dark, and my client was riding without front and rear bike lights, which are required by Virginia law. Before he hired me, several other lawyers told him his case was a loser because he was contributorily negligent for riding without lights. But it turns out they were wrong.

Why? Because upon further investigation we determined that he was struck immediately adjacent to a used car lot that was lit up with mercury vapor lights. The entire area was as bright as a major league ballpark, and his bike was plainly visible to the SUV regardless of whether he was riding with lights or not. In other words, although he was negligent, he was not *contributorily negligent* because his failure to use lights *did not contribute* to the cause of the accident. Using some clear nighttime photos of the scene, we managed to secure a very healthy settlement for this young man.

If the doctrine of contributory negligence sounds harsh and unreasonable, it is. But it is the law in Virginia, Maryland, DC, North Carolina, and Alabama, and the insurance companies profit handsomely from it. This is why their adjusters and lawyers will do everything they can to find that **one little thing you might have done wrong** that contributed to the accident. One little thing is all they need to make a case for contributory negligence. BE CAREFUL WHAT YOU SAY!!

CHAPTER 14

OKAY, I'VE RETAINED A QUALIFIED LAWYER. HOW DOES THE PROCESS WORK? DO WE FILE A LAWSUIT RIGHT AWAY? DOES MY CASE HAVE TO GO TO COURT?

Stage One: Case Preparation

Once retained, the first step in the process is for your attorney to begin a thorough investigation of the accident, both factually and legally. Depending on the circumstances, your attorney may notify the assigned insurance adjuster that he or she is representing you in the matter of your claim right away.[12] This is accomplished informally by a call placed to the adjuster, and then followed up formally with the attorney sending a "letter of representation" (otherwise known as a "letter of rep") confirming the fact that you are now represented by counsel. Once that happens, the adjuster should cease attempting to contact you and will deal directly with your attorney.

If you continue to receive calls, inform the adjuster that all communications should be through your attorney and politely cease further communications. They will get the message.

[12] Like most things in the law, however, not always. If the other driver has been cited with a traffic infraction in connection with the accident, for example, some plaintiffs' attorneys may choose to stay in the background while that process plays out.

Note that I have emphasized more than once that you should be polite when dealing with adjusters over the phone at all times. Being rude or argumentative is never an effective way to advance your position, and will only serve to characterize you (perhaps accurately), as a "hot head." And if your adjuster thinks you are a "hot head," he or she will know that if the case is headed for trial, you are not likely to be an attractive witness to the jury, and may value your case accordingly for settlement purposes. So do yourself (and your lawyer) a favor. Be civil and controlled at all times when speaking with adjusters or other insurance company representatives. Your appearance as a potential witness in your case begins from the very first conversation you have with that adjuster.

The next step is for your attorney to meet with you and conduct a detailed, fact-finding interview to learn as much as humanly possible about the facts and circumstances of the accident, and your resulting injuries. Hopefully, you may have witness contact information, perhaps a police report, and even better, perhaps photographs – both of the accident scene and of you following your injuries. In addition, you will be asked to sign a medical information release so that your attorney can obtain all medical bills and records pertaining to your treatment, as well as any related to preexisting injuries should you have any. Hopefully, you will be able to provide your attorney with the names and addresses of all treating physicians, or at the very least, the hospitals where you were treated for your injuries, and any follow up visits, including physical therapy where applicable.

It is important to remember that the attorney's ability to thoroughly investigate the case relies heavily upon your honesty and complete cooperation. Be patient with the level of detail that your lawyer inquires about, and hold nothing back in your communications regarding any and all aspects of the accident and treatment, including your past medical history. If there is something you think could be harmful to your case, whatever it is, TELL YOUR LAWYER ABOUT IT AS SOON AS POSSIBLE. It is essential that your lawyer have all relevant information, so let your attorney decide what is relevant and what is not. When in doubt, err on the side of complete and full disclosure. If you don't, what you don't tell your lawyer now *could* -- and probably *will* come back to damage or even wreck your case later on.

Stage Two: Physical Investigation of the Scene

In many cases, the foundational issue of liability may be an issue, either through contributory negligence or otherwise. In such cases, it is important that any applicable physical evidence be evaluated and preserved if possible, and if not, effectively documented. For example, skid mark intensity and length may be a factor in a case, but can be worn away in short order depending on traffic and weather conditions.

A good lawyer will either personally or have a trained investigator visit the scene immediately and take high quality photographs and video to bolster your testimony at trial as to what happened and when. A single photo of a skid mark can make or break a case, as can photographs of overhanging tree limbs that affect visibility, high grass growing in a median strip that may soon be mowed, etc. Similarly, if the accident took place at or near a road construction site (a common scenario in bicycle accidents), the physical appearance of the scene could change drastically in as little as a single day. This is especially common in summer months when road construction and maintenance activity is commonplace. Lastly, you should photograph the physical condition of your bicycle immediately after the accident, focusing on damaged parts and frame components, and perhaps even hold off on having it repaired depending upon how the claim develops.[13]

The best advice here is, when it comes to investigating the accident: "get on it," and quickly. Any delay can result in loss of evidence that could be critical to the success of your case.

Stage Three: Treatment and Documentation of Injuries

By now, you know that getting immediate and timely medical attention for your injuries is extremely important. Keep a journal of your doctor visits and treatment, as well as a log of personal expenditures related to your treatment, including prescription and non-prescription drugs. While your attorney will likely assemble your medical records and bills independently, your independent journal detailing treatments, including your own personal perceptions of

[13] If your bike has been damaged, take it to a reputable local bike shop and have them provide a written estimate of the damages, or replacement value if the frame has been compromised. Make sure the estimate is signed and is on the bike shop's letterhead, so your attorney can present it to the insurance company in support of your property damages claim.

progress, will be extremely valuable in preparing your case. It is absolutely worth doing.

If you are losing time from work, be sure to record the dates and times in your journal, and document the reason for your time away from work with your employer. If it is appropriate to make a lost wage claim in your case, appropriate documentation of your time away from your employer will be extremely helpful, if not essential to justify compensation. And I am not just talking about time in addition to your accrued/ used sick leave. Rather, I am talking about every minute that you are out of work as a result of your injuries, whether for initial treatment or subsequent follow up visits with your doctor, including physical therapy. Record it *all*, and provide copies of your notes to your attorney on a regular basis. In addition, request a letter from your employer documenting the time missed from work, and why, as well as confirmation of your salary or hourly rate of pay. Like every other aspect of your case, the insurance company will *not* "take your word for it" without thorough documentation.

Stage Four: Settlement Discussions

Throughout this process, you should have periodic conversations with your attorney to keep him or her apprised as to your anticipated course of treatment, and how well you are doing. This is essential for two reasons. First, it will help your lawyer plan accordingly in terms of timing settlement negotiations and the possible filing of a lawsuit, if necessary. In Virginia, suit must be filed within two years from the date of injury. After that, your suit is barred by the "statute of limitations," which exists for a number of policy reasons, one of which is to ensure that evidence is reasonably fresh and reliable.[14]

Second, this ongoing information on your treatment will be relevant to periodic discussions between your attorney and the insurance adjuster assigned to your claim. Depending on the severity of your injuries, insurance companies are required by law to set aside certain financial "reserves" to ensure that adequate cash is available to pay likely, pending claims. If you withhold information in a case of severe injuries thinking that somehow "surprising" the adjuster with a big claim later will have some sort of beneficial effect, the reverse could be true. Making it possible for the carrier to set aside sufficient reserves early on can sometimes facilitate settlement discussions within an appropriate range.

At some point, ideally when you have made sufficient progress to reach "MMI" or "maximum medial improvement," it is time for your lawyer to engage in serious settlement discussions with the insurance carrier for the responsible party. By now, your attorney will likely have a recommendation as to how much to "demand." In this case, the word has a formal, legal meaning, and refers to the amount requested on your behalf

---

[14] Another, and indeed primary reason for the statute of limitations, is to impose a measure of finality with respect to outstanding legal claims. Applicable statutes of limitations vary considerably on a state-by-state basis, and also vary depending upon the nature of the legal claim involved. For example, an accident claim based upon negligence may not be subject to the same statute of limitations as a claim for breach of contract, etc.

to settle the claim. If it is too low, the level of compensation ultimately paid out may be lower than what you are entitled to. On the other hand, if it is absurdly high, it will bring about a quick end to settlement discussions, eliminating all possibility of satisfactorily resolving the matter short of going to trial. It may also telegraph a message to the adjuster that your attorney doesn't now what he or she is doing, which of course is not a good message to send.

How much do I "demand"? If your have chosen your lawyer correctly, you should demand the amount that your lawyer recommends. Remember that recommendation will be based upon years of experience evaluating and settling cases, and knowing what a jury is likely to do if you opt to go to trial (more on this in a moment). I've seen many clients balk when they hear a proposed settlement from a lawyer, because emotionally they expected a number far higher than their injuries and the circumstances reasonably justify. Or worse, they are listening to their "friends," who, although they have no knowledge or real experience in the field, are more than happy to share their opinions about what they think your case is worth, based upon faulty ideas that your case is "just like" some other case they may know about through friends, family, or even television. As we've already discussed, anyone who tells you that is sadly misinformed.

At this stage, it is helpful to remind yourself why you retained an experienced bike lawyer in the first instance. Was it to provide you with sound, experienced legal advice? Hopefully, the answer is a resounding "yes." So remember that fact when considering your lawyer's advice on how much to demand in terms of an initial offer, and allow the process to begin accordingly. In the end, you will be glad that you did.

When the lawyer has your approval as to the amount of the demand, a demand package will be sent, including a detailed "demand letter" prepared by the lawyer, along with all applicable medical bills and records. At this point, the timing depends upon the complexity of the case, and the workload of the adjuster. Well formulated, complete packages get to the top of the assigned adjuster's pile fastest. Incomplete packages with missing bills and records go to the bottom of the pile. Once again, the experience of your attorney in knowing what to say and what to send in these packages is critical to the process.

Given that most adjusters have a heavy caseload, some time may pass before your demand package can be evaluated. Assuming the adjuster recognizes that there is some cognizable basis for liability in the case, an initial settlement offer will be made and negotiations will ensue. Although there are no hard and fast rules on how negotiations will proceed (and a lot will depend upon your lawyer's preferred approach to this process), things could progress quickly. If the parties can reach mutual ground, a settlement can be agreed upon. Thereafter, a settlement check will be prepared and forwarded to your attorney, as well as a written "release of liability" that you will be asked to sign releasing the other driver (and the insurer) from any further liability in the case. Your attorney should review the "release" to be sure that the terms are reasonable, and answer any and all questions you may have about the settlement before you sign it. Remember – once you sign the release and the check is cashed, the claim is over. Absent exceptional circumstances, there is no going back.

If you have agreed to settle, then congratulations. Let me say a few words about the process of collecting and distributing the money, because there is definitely a standard approach here that most personal injury attorneys employ and you should be aware of it.

With respect to the actual settlement proceeds, most attorneys have a provision in their fee agreements stating that any settlement check will be made out both to the client, and to the attorney. Do not be concerned about this practice. It is a standard, acceptable procedure that most insurance companies follow.[15] Once you and your attorney have endorsed the settlement check, it is typically deposited into the lawyer's client "trust account," and once it clears, the lawyer disburses the proceeds of the settlement to the client, minus the attorneys fees, costs of settlement, and any liens that may exist with respect to the settlement money. In Virginia, for example, unpaid doctors, hospitals and other medical providers that provided treatment to you for your injuries may have a statutory "lien" for certain amounts if their bills

[15] One common exception is when the carrier agrees to settle the property damages portion of an injured cyclist's claim prior to settling the claim for bodily injuries. Usually, the carrier will issue a check directly to the client, in the client's name only. Whether your lawyer is entitled to his or her contingent fee percentage of the property damages compensation depends on the terms of your fee agreement.

have not been paid.[16] By law, your attorney is obligated to honor these liens if the providers gave the proper notice, and is obligated to ensure that they are satisfied before disbursing the proceeds to you.

Section Five: No Acceptable Settlement? The Pros and Cons of Filing Suit.

If your attorney has not been able to negotiate an acceptable settlement offer from the adjuster, then it may be necessary to proceed with filing a civil lawsuit for negligence, and possibly other legal theories of liability. These bases for liability are referred to as "causes of action" under the law. This may also be necessary if, regardless of where you are in your settlement negotiations, the statute of limitations in your jurisdiction is getting close to running out and you must file suit to preserve your rights to do so.

If the statute of limitations is the only issue and you are still making headway with your case, then depending on the rules of your jurisdiction, you may be able to file suit but still keep the case in the hands of the adjuster (rather than having it transferred over to the hands of the insurance company's lawyers). This is done by not actually "serving" the defendant with "process" (i.e., the lawsuit summons) in order to keep the case essentially on hold while you continue to negotiate.

[16] Virginia Code Section 8.01-66.2.

Some states allow you to do this and some do not, depending on the applicable laws and court procedural rules for where you need to file suit. The location of the jurisdiction where you would file the case is known in legal speak as the case "venue," and is generally the county where the accident took place, although other considerations might make it more strategically advantageous to file the case elsewhere if possible.

The disadvantage of filing suit unnecessarily is that if the adjuster is negotiating in good faith, you may be able to secure a reasonable settlement and receive your compensation a lot sooner than if you rush to file a lawsuit. Once suit is filed, the adjuster hands the case off to defense counsel (the insurance company's in-house or outside hired law firm), and once that happens, those lawyers will typically want to proceed through a months long "discovery process" before settlement discussions can reconvene, if at all. (For more on legal "discovery" once suit is filed, see Chapter 15).

Sometimes, however, filing a lawsuit is simply unavoidable. If the adjuster is proceeding in bad faith, or otherwise intentionally delaying the process, you are simply wasting time and playing into the insurance company's hands by prolonging discussions with someone who isn't serious about resolving your claim. Many insurance companies instruct their adjusters to intentionally delay payment as long as possible. An experienced lawyer will recognize this strategy pretty quickly, and advise you accordingly.

Section Six: Are There Alternatives To Court? What about mediation? What is arbitration?

Going to trial is often not the only option available to resolve the cyclist's claim. In many cases, both parties will attempt to "mediate" the case, and the mediation process often produces excellent results for both sides. There are many misconceptions about mediation, however, so let's understand a few important principles about it for you to consider.

Mediation:

First of all, mediation is a **voluntary** process whereby the parties agree to meet with a mediator (often a retired judge or a trained mediator with expertise in the field). The purpose of the meeting is to try and hammer out a voluntary settlement that both sides can live with. Note that I said "voluntary" because the mediator does not order one party to pay the other. In fact, the mediator cannot order either party to do anything at all. What the mediator *can* do, however, is talk to both parties (usually together at first, and then separately during a subsequent "back and forth" offer / counter offer process), and in so doing, lend some experience and guidance to the negotiation. In my experience, it can be an extremely productive process.

If the parties agree to mediation,[17] and the mediation does not produce a settlement, the case can continue to trial. All that is lost is the time, effort, and if a private mediator is used, the

---

[17] Some courts actually require the parties to submit to court-ordered mediation as a prerequisite to obtaining a trial date.

fees associated with using the mediation service.[18] Typically, the parties agree in advance to split the mediator's fee.

Usually however, if both parties agree to engage in the mediation process in good faith, it produces a settlement. In this way, **the parties themselves maintain control over the outcome**, instead of delegating it to a group of strangers in a jury box, whose sole qualification to decide your case is that they registered to vote. If you find that fact a little scary, you should. Once both parties hand their case over to a jury, they have, by definition, lost control of the outcome.

Arbitration:

Another process, often confused with mediation, is arbitration. This is a process whereby both sides agree to hire the services of a trained arbitrator, who essentially sits as judge and jury, and decides the case one way or the other instead of a trial by jury in a court. In arbitration, the arbitrator can and will order one party to pay the other if liability and damages are proven to the arbitrator's satisfaction. The process usually takes less time and money to accomplish than litigation in court, but in the end, absent exceptional circumstances (fraud, etc.), the parties have to live with the arbitrator's decision. It is

[18] Often the mediator is paid an hourly fee comparable to those charged by a substantial law firm. There are usually also facility charges as well if the parties use the conference rooms made available by the mediation service. Sometimes these facility charges can be avoided if the parties agree to meet at the law offices of one party's lawyers.

binding by law, the same as a court judgment, and is enforceable in court if the parties refuse to abide by the decision. But unlike a trial by jury in a court of law, there is no appeal. The result is final.

CHAPTER 15

IF WE HAVE TO FILE A LAWSUIT, WHAT HAPPENS AND WHEN?

If your claim cannot be effectively negotiated to a successful settlement, your lawyer will discuss with you what is involved in filing a lawsuit. Every case is different, but a typical personal injury lawsuit for negligence happens as follows:

1. Filing Suit

The beginning of any lawsuit involves filing a "complaint," which is a formal legal document (otherwise referred to as a "pleading") that your lawyer will prepare on your behalf. It should consist of short, numbered paragraphs detailing the identity of the parties, the jurisdiction of the court, the amount being sought, the legal basis for the claim, and the essential facts to be proven by the plaintiff in support of that claim. The length of the document may vary depending upon the circumstances of the case, the legal theories of recovery, the complexity of the facts, and the number of parties. Typically, your attorney will review a draft of the complaint with you carefully before filing it with the court to make sure that the facts stated in the document are correct.

After the "complaint" is filed with the court, it has to be "served" upon the negligent party (now referred to as the "defendant"). This is also called "service of process." Usually, the service can be handled in one of two ways, either through the local sheriff's office, or through use of a private, professional "process server" who takes the complaint, along with a document issued by the court clerk's office called a "summons," and "serves" it on the defendant. There are very specific rules about how this is to be done, and those rules vary by state and local jurisdiction.[19] In addition, there are rules and laws about when "service" has to be accomplished. In Virginia, for example, it has to be done within one year of when the lawsuit is filed.

2. Discovery

If the defendant has been served, and has insurance, then that insurance company will assign the case to an "insurance defense" lawyer who will take over the responsibility of defending the defendant. The first thing that is done is the filing of a pleading by the defendant called an "Answer," which responds to the specific allegations of the complaint. Like the complaint itself, it is usually a relatively short document and does not contain much detail. In order for both sides to find out more detail about the other's position in the case, they engage in a process known as "discovery."

"Discovery" involves a number of different things, but typically includes at least three parts: "interrogatories," "requests for production of documents," and "depositions."

[19] For example, some states require the documents to actually be physically handed to the defendant. Others permit service by "posting" (i.e., by affixing the documents to the defendant's door at his/her house or apartment if he/she isn't at home).

3. Interrogatories

Interrogatories are formal written questions that are submitted by one party to the other, and there is a time limitation on answering them – usually 21 or 30 days depending on the jurisdiction, though lawyers often grant each other informal extensions of time if they need it. As with everything else involving a lawsuit, there are specific and detailed laws and rules that govern the entire discovery process, including interrogatories. These specify the number of questions that can be asked, and the subject matter that they can go into. The ultimate goal, on both sides, is to get answers to as many detailed questions as possible, in order to "discover" or find out as much as they can about the other side's case in advance of trial. In most jurisdictions, answers to interrogatories must be signed and "sworn to" under oath and penalty of perjury, much the same as if you were testifying under oath in a court of law.

If you are the plaintiff in a personal injury case, your attorney will help you with responding to these interrogatories, and may also assist with the actual wording. There is nothing wrong with your attorney assisting in this process, and believe me, you will want your lawyer's help, as the number and complexity of the questions can be intimidating. A good lawyer will simplify the process, and help you complete your interrogatory responses as efficiently as possible. Your attorney will also know when to formally object to one or more of the interrogatories as being out of bounds under the applicable rules of court.

4. Request For Production of Documents

Frequently, along with their interrogatories, the defendant will serve the plaintiff with a "request for production of documents." In a typical accident case, the defendant will most certainly request all of the plaintiff's medical records and bills pertaining to treatment for the injuries sustained in the accident, as well as documents pertaining to any lost wages claim that might be part of the case. Some attorneys will shoulder the heavy lifting on obtaining all of these documents from your medical providers. Others will expect you to do most of the work. (And believe me, it is work! You would be amazed at how uncooperative some doctors' offices, hospitals and clinics can be when they receive requests for bills and records. It often takes a lot of patience, letter writing and telephone calling to gather everything up in a timely fashion.)

5. Depositions

Depositions are normally (but not always) taken after the interrogatory and "document request" part of the discovery are concluded. They are normally conducted in the lawyers' offices and involve a formal process whereby the lawyers get to ask questions of the opposing parties and any potential witnesses in the case. The witnesses are sworn to tell the truth (under penalty of perjury), and everything that is said is taken down verbatim by a court reporter, who produces a written transcript. Each side pays for the transcripts that they order from the court reporter in any given deposition. These reporters generally charge by the page. In some cases, these transcripts can be fairly expensive, and often, their cost comprises one of the larger costs that you may be responsible for paying as a "cost" of suit. (For more on "costs" versus "fees," see Chapter 9.)

Many witnesses are nervous about about going through the deposition process, which is understandable, because unless you have been a witness in a lawsuit before, there is no reason why you would have ever had this experience. This is why it is absolutely essential that your attorney take the time necessary to go over your testimony in detail, take you through a "dry run" of the deposition in advance so that you get used to answering the questions, and otherwise prepare you thoroughly for having your deposition taken. Time and again, I've seen sloppy lawyers simply tell their clients to show up 15 minutes early to "go over a few ground rules" just before they have their deposition taken. This is <u>not</u> sufficient preparation, and more often than not is a prescription for disaster.

In my opinion, the best way to prepare is for you and your attorney to set aside an appropriate period of time, usually no more than a day or two before the deposition, to thoroughly prepare you. That way, on the day of your deposition, all facts will be fresh in your mind, and you will be confident, knowledgeable, and thoroughly prepared to come across as an effective witness. If you hit the ball out of the park in your deposition, you may have paved your way to a quick settlement.

Why is thorough preparation for your deposition so important? Well, first of all, because, your answers matter a great deal. If the case goes to trial, and your testimony at trial differs from your testimony in the deposition (say, as to how the accident happened or the nature of your injuries), the defense lawyer will call you out on it in front of the jury, damaging your credibility. In legal speak, this is called "impeaching" witnesses, and it can be devastating to your case. Even if it is over small issues, a jury may figure that if you are lying or exaggerating the small stuff, you may be doing the same on the larger issues as well.

Secondly, the purpose of the deposition is not only so the lawyer can learn all of the facts in your case… it is also to size you up as a witness. Are your answers articulate and precise? Or are they vague and confusing? Do you come across as a sincere, responsible person who has suffered real injuries? Or as a whiner who is exaggerating their claim? Do you answer the questions put to you clearly or vaguely? How does your "body language" come across: open and honest or closed and evasive? Do you have a defensive attitude and resist answering even the easiest question in plain English? What would that attitude convey to a jury with power to decide whether and/or how much you deserve to be compensated for your injuries?

These are all factors that relate to your preparation, and are all factors that the defense lawyer will be taking into account when he advises his "boss" (the insurance company adjuster) about how the deposition went. If he says you were a "good witness," then good for you. You just increased the likelihood that your case might settle in an appropriate range. If the defense counsel reports that you are a "bad witness" (argumentative, defensive, inarticulate, exaggerating), the insurance company will have a lot less incentive to settle the case, and may be more than happy to take the case to trial, knowing from your performance at the deposition that you are not likely to come across well to a jury and that the jury will award you little, if anything.

Good, thorough deposition preparation is absolutely essential, and good lawyers will insist on it. It will take some time, but know that it is well worth it, so you should cooperate fully. And if you hear "just show up a few minutes early before your deposition so we can go over a few questions," you should know **that isn't enough.** Insist that your lawyer take the time necessary to make sure you are properly prepared. "Relax, just tell the truth and be yourself" may be good advice for a first date, but it is not a prescription for success in having your deposition taken – it is a prescription for a train wreck. Telling the truth is mandatory, but it is not enough. Knowing *how* to answer the questions asked is important, and is a learnable skill. Good preparation should always include a "dry run" through questions you will surely get, so that you won't be hearing them from opposing counsel for the first time on the day of your deposition. In summary, thorough preparation includes experienced advice on how to answer questions that are sure to be asked, in a way that doesn't harm your case but is still truthful and honest. **[TIP: For a list of basic deposition guidelines that my clients have found useful, see Appendix 4 at the end of this book. But remember, these guidelines are no substitute for thorough, one-on-one preparation between you and your attorney the day before your deposition. Insist on it.]**

6. Trial

As the plaintiff, you bear the "burden of proof "at trial. This legal term means that you must prove it is more likely than not 1) that the defendant driver was negligent, and 2) that such negligence directly caused your injuries, or "damages." Both testimony and documentary evidence are introduced by both sides, and ultimately, the case is submitted to the jury (or, in cases that are "bench trials," the case is submitted to the judge for decision). The length of the trial depends upon the number of witnesses, the quantity of documentation, and the overall complexity of the case. Some personal injury trials last half a day, and others can last more than a week, though in my personal experience most personal injury trials are concluded in two days or less.

Whether it is prudent to go forward with a trial depends on numerous factors that you and your attorney should discuss carefully and objectively. Because all cases are different, there are no standard considerations that apply in all circumstances. Nevertheless, when evaluating your options, the following questions should be discussed with your attorney:

- What are the most significant legal and factual issues in my case?
- How is a jury likely to view those issues?[20]

[20] This assumes that your case will be tried before a jury, which may not be the case. In the Commonwealth of Virginia, where I happen to have a lot of my cases, claims for $25,000 and under are generally tried in the General District Court. In General District Court, cases are tried before a single judge, not a jury. This is often an important consideration, and where applicable, should be discussed with your attorney.

- How are my witnesses likely to be viewed by the jury?
- How are the other side's witnesses likely to be viewed by a jury?
- What, in the lawyer's experience, is the likely potential range of award assuming that liability can be established?
- Is that estimate based upon a review of recent published jury verdicts in the applicable jurisdiction? What is the published range in our jurisdiction (part of the country)?
- How heavy is the applicable court's docket calendar (trial schedule)? In other words, how long will it be before I have a trial date? When is the case likely to go to trial? In six months? A year's time? Two years?
- What, in the lawyer's view, are the biggest risks and rewards in going to trial?
- What will it cost me in expenses to go to trial? (Even if your attorney is on a contingent fee, if you have serious injuries, you will want one or more of your treating doctors to testify, and as we discussed earlier, that may cost you thousands in expert witness fees up front, with no guarantee of recovery.)

These are all complex issues, with no "black and white" answers. Accordingly, it is important for both the attorney and the client to approach this analysis honestly, carefully and <u>objectively</u>. This isn't easy, especially if you have been badly hurt by the carelessness of another. Anger and resentment toward the negligent party are understandable, but **don't let**

these emotions affect your decision about going to trial. When your objectivity is replaced with anger and frustration, you can end up making a bad decision that you may regret later.

Ultimately, if you have confidence in your case and your attorney, and the other side isn't being close to reasonable in their settlement offer, then you may indeed wish to proceed with trial. But if you do, remember the following:

Once your case is submitted to the jury at the end of the trial, you have lost all final control over the outcome. Neither side has any further say in how the case turns out. It is entirely in the hands of strangers, whose sole qualification to determine your case is that they registered to vote. Some people, when they consider that fact, find it a little scary. That's because it is. Juries are unpredictable, and that is a fact of life no matter how strong your case may seem.

It is always helpful to keep in mind that nothing the jury does by way of a verdict can put you back the way you were before your accident. That bell has been rung. They can award you money, but they can never undo all the pain and mental anguish that you have suffered as a result of your accident. One of our finest mediators here in Virginia, a well-regarded retired judge, frequently reminds parties of that fact if they are having difficulty reaching a settlement. It is sad, but true, and worth remembering when you are weighing the pros and cons of rolling the dice down at the courthouse.

CHAPTER 16

COMMON BICYCLE ACCIDENTS AND HOW TO AVOID THEM

There are many ways to get into a bike accident. While the contributing circumstances are many, over the years I've definitely seen a pattern. Most bike accidents fall into one or more of the following categories – and many can be avoided if you ride defensively and know what to look for. Before we look at these categories, though, let's talk about sound "riding style" or philosophy.

Reasonable minds can differ on the subject, but riding styles are generally defined in two ways. The first way is the "offensive" style, whereby the cyclist is well aware of his/her rights as a vehicle on the roadway, and behaves accordingly. The offensive rider tends to ride closer to the center of the lane, always stops in the center at lights and stop signs, and gives no ground. From this perspective, cars should recognize the rights of the cyclist "come hell or high water," and it is better to be conspicuous and visible than to timidly keep to the far right and pray no one takes you out. "I know my rights on the road" is the battle cry of the offensive cyclist, and they ride as if they are spoiling for a fight with every motorist who doesn't show them the respect they feel they deserve.

The second style is purely defensive in nature. The defensive cyclist rides under the assumption that he or she is invisible to all other vehicles on the road. The defensive cyclist assumes every driver is looking elsewhere, and will place the cyclist in harm's way whenever possible. When it comes to anticipating the behavior of cars and pedestrians they encounter, defensive cyclists assume the worst will happen, and plan accordingly.

In my experience, most riders are somewhere in the middle of these two styles. While neither approach is absolutely right or absolutely wrong, my personal philosophy leans in favor of the defensive approach. Whenever possible, I constantly play the "what if" game as I ride when observing other cars on the road. What if that guy turns right in front of me without signaling? Where can I bail out to avoid a wreck? What if that oncoming car making the left turn doesn't see me? Is there a path to safety if he doesn't? Playing the "what if" game when you ride takes discipline and practice, but it has saved my hide countless times. If it works for me, it can work for you. It has so far, anyway.

Sooner or later, if you ride on the road enough you are likely to encounter one or more of these common accident scenarios. Here they are, along with tips on how to avoid them.

The Left Hook

This is hands down, the most common accident scenario in road cycling (and motorcycling too, by the way). A left-turning vehicle fails to yield to the oncoming cyclist in the opposite lane, and either runs the cyclist down outright, or the cyclist collides with the turning vehicle's front passenger side fender.

Inevitably, the driver will admit that he just "never saw" the cyclist, or claim it was the cyclist's fault because he/she "just came out of nowhere" and must have been riding too fast. Typically, of course, neither is true. The cyclist didn't "come out of nowhere," they were visible in their approach the entire time. And they probably weren't exceeding the speed limit either. What causes these accidents is the simple fact that the human brain often fails to "see" smaller objects like bicycles because it is really on the lookout for cars, trucks and buses.

The way to avoid these accidents is simple. **NEVER ASSUME AN ONCOMING LEFT TURNING VEHICLE CAN SEE YOU.** And forget that stuff about "making eye contact" unless the motorist specifically waives you forward. They may have eye contact with you and they may not. So ride accordingly. Have a bail out option. And if one isn't available, slow up and let the turning vehicle complete their turn. It may slow down the flow of your ride, but it could save you a nasty crash as well.

The Right Hook

This is the second most common scenario, and can be devastating. A car passes a cyclist on the left, and then makes a right hand turn directly into the path of the cyclist without signaling or otherwise checking their right hand mirror to make sure the coast is clear. I never cease to be amazed at how drivers can "forget" about the presence of a slower moving cyclist they just passed mere seconds before making that right hand turn directly into the cyclist's path. In my view, it comes back to the brain's non-recognition of the cyclist. The driver is capable of seeing the cyclist, but it just doesn't register in his or her cognitive thought.

The T-Bone

The third most common wreck is when the cyclist simply rides out into a roadway from a cross street or driveway, and fails to yield to the cross traffic. In most cases, this is a "failure to yield" scenario on the part of the cyclist, not the car, and fault will almost always rest with the cyclist in terms of a claim for damages. It should go without saying that before entering any roadway, stop, look and wait as long as necessary to make a safe entry into the flow. Your life depends on it.

The Oncoming Right Hook

This is the reverse scenario when a motorist makes a right hand turn (either green light or right-turn-on-red) and strikes an oncoming cyclist riding in the opposite direction against the flow of traffic. Legally, who is at fault here will depend heavily on the circumstances, but from a safety standpoint, riding against the flow of traffic is never a good idea. If you are on a sidewalk, and riding on the sidewalk is legal in that jurisdiction, you may have the legal *right* to do it. But that doesn't mean it's a smart thing to do. A general rule of thumb is to *always ride in the direction of traffic if at all possible.* And if you cannot, you'd better give the benefit of the doubt to other cars, and ride like you're invisible. In this situation, you might as well be, in terms of the likelihood that they will be looking out for you.

Passing Motorist

This happens when a passing motorist simply misjudges the distance between his passenger side door and the cyclist, and "clips" the cyclist with his mirror. It can also happen when the motorist misjudges when the cyclist has actually been fully overtaken, and moves back to the right prematurely. In these cases, the cyclist is typically thrown to the right, either off the road completely, or into a nasty crash in the gutter.

Avoiding these crashes is difficult, but it helps if you maintain a steady "line" of travel, and avoid sudden swerves or moves to the left that can cause unintended contact with an overtaking vehicle. It also helps to be aware of the road ahead. If you are approaching a blind curve or the rest of a hill, it may make sense to take a bit more of the lane, encouraging the car behind to wait until visibility is restored and they can pass you safely without having to cut it too close.

Getting "Doored"

These crashes happen to urban cyclists all the time, and can cause horrific injuries. It is amazing how normally careful drivers just don't think to look first before they throw a driver's side door open – especially when parking on streets where there is a designated bike lane!

Ideally, the way to avoid these crashes is to imagine the swinging width of a car door, and maintain a safe distance from it. In busy traffic, however, this is often easier said than done. When I am riding in an urban area, I always keep a sharp eye out for the driver's side seats on all parked cars. If there is someone in that seat, I assume their sole purpose in life is to kill me by swinging the door open at the last instant. Ride defensively.

GENERAL RIDING TIPS TO KEEP YOU OUT OF TROUBLE

Think About Your Route and Plan Ahead

We are all creatures of habit. If you drive to work, do you take the same route every day? The chances are, you probably do. But should you take the same route on a bike? Not necessarily. If there are options you can take to minimize your contact with dense traffic, then take them. It is just common sense. The fact is that while it may be legal to ride just about anywhere, many roads simply aren't safe for cyclists – either because of the speed of the traffic flow, the number of cars and intersections, or the large proximity of parked cars. The busier the street, the greater the risk.

Many bike groups and clubs in urban areas publish bike commuter maps that help cyclists plan their safest routes in and out of the city. While some of these routes may appear to add distance to your commute, they may save you time in the long run due to more predictable traffic flow. Check out the web for bike advocacy groups in your jurisdiction that make these maps and resources available. It is well worth the effort.

Speaking of bike routes, let me add a few points about using GPS devices designed for bikes. Recent advancements in technology have made these devices increasingly affordable, and they are terrific training and navigation tools. In heavy traffic, however, they can be highly dangerous because they divert the cyclist's attention from the surroundings. Just as texting and cell phone use can be a dangerous distraction to a motorist, GPS devices on handlebar mounts can be just as distracting and dangerous to a cyclist. Use them sparingly and wisely, and in heavy traffic, KEEP YOUR EYES ON THE ROAD. If you are lost, pull over to a safe place while you figure out where you are.

Be Flexible With Your Lane Position

"Lane position" refers to your relative position in the traffic lane, be it on the left, middle or right hand side. Safe lane positioning is a skill that comes from experience, and there is no one position to be in that will ensure your safety under all circumstances. The important thing is to be aware and fully conscious of where you are in the lane at all times, and maintain a consistent "line" so that your position is predictable to the traffic around you. But don't be stubborn about it. Varying traffic, weather and other factors should dictate how much lane you take up, and when. Be smart. Be flexible. You need to be willing to adapt your position to the circumstances presented.

In many states, the law requires you to stay generally to the right side of the lane. My personal rule of thumb is: if traffic is moving considerably faster than you, keep about a foot to the left of the right hand lane marker. If you are going about the same speed as the traffic flow, you may want to take up a bit more lane to avoid getting squeezed into the gutter. What you should never do, however, is ride fast *and* close to the curb at the same time, passing cars on the right at high speed. If you do that through intersections, you are begging for a dangerous "right hook." By the time you see a car pulling out to make a right hand turn in front of you, it will be too late to avoid a crash.

Several years ago, I had a client who was outraged at the fact that he had been right hooked, and even more outraged when the insurance carrier for the driver refused to accept liability, forcing him to file an expensive and time consuming lawsuit to recover for his injuries and bike damage. When I reviewed the facts of the case with him, he mentioned with astonishment that he had nearly been "right-hooked" in similar fashion no less than three times *on the same street* just minutes before the fourth time that finally took him out. What does that tell you about his defensive riding skills? What he thought was just bad luck was a predictable result of his own poor riding judgment and inexperience. His accident could have been avoided had he slowed down a bit and been more cautious.

Special Treatment For Larger, Heavy Vehicles

If a vehicle weighs over 5 tons (like a truck or bus), my advice is to assume it cannot see you. Even with lots of side view and convex mirrors, drivers of these larger vehicles have a lot to keep track of, so "ride like you're invisible" because to them, you probably are! And while we are at it, the same goes for anything with a trailer, whether it's a truck, car, or a large tractor-trailer. As a former tractor-trailer driver myself, I can attest to the truth of what I am telling you.

Stop At All Red Lights and Stop Signs, and Always Yield to Pedestrians in Crosswalks

I am always amazed at cyclists who love to sound off about how they have all the legal **rights** of other vehicles, but ignore the ***responsibilities*** that other vehicles have – like obeying the traffic laws. Obeying the law is every cyclist's responsibility, and by doing it, you not only protect yourself, but you set a good example out there on the road. It is hard to criticize drivers (who are also jurors, insurance adjusters, and police officers, by the way) for treating cyclists as "second class citizens" when those same cyclists *ride* like second class citizens by ignoring basic traffic laws. So do yourself and your fellow cyclists a favor – set the bar high for your own conduct on the road. It pays big dividends to your personal safety, and to the cycling community at large.

Don't Lose Your Cool With Offensive Motorists – Ever

Every cyclist who rides knows there are motorists out there who are completely clueless when comes to respecting bicycles on the road. They cut you off, take you down, and seemingly try to kill you with their carelessness and inattention. Maddening, isn't it?

Of course. As human beings, we have all been angered, suddenly and intensely, when a driver does something to endanger us. Our adrenaline peaks, our heart rate soars, and all to often, all we can think about is chasing down that driver and telling him or her what they've just done. We want to tell them they are idiots, and that they can't behave that way.

Well, don't do it. Ever.

Why? Because *you have no idea who that person is, and what they are capable of.* They could be a convicted felon with a history of violence carrying a weapon. They could be a schizophrenic off their medication, a manic depressive having a bad day, a drunk or drug addict who is DUI, or a combination of all these things. **Yelling at the driver can only put you in danger**, and accomplishes nothing. Refrain from "going after them" at all costs.

If you've been the victim of an aggressive driver, take down their plate number and make/model of car, and notify the police. It is better to have been a victim once than a victim twice.

CHAPTER 17

SIX MISTAKES THAT CAN SERIOUSLY HURT YOUR BICYCLE CASE

(OR HOW TO DRIVE YOUR LAWYER INSANE AND DESTROY YOUR CASE IN THE PROCESS: WHAT NOT TO DO)

Like members of any profession, personal injury attorneys share their experiences from time to time, and compare notes about memorable cases and clients. Without breaching confidentiality, I've learned that some clients tend to do things, often repeatedly, that frustrate their attorneys to no end, and definitely impair the attorney-client relationship. In some cases, I've seen things get so bad that the lawyer actually "fires" the client who is literally making that lawyer's life miserable.

Here are some examples of things that a small minority of clients feel are appropriate, and which are sure to inflict damage on their relationships with their lawyers.

1. **Call your lawyer every time a question pops into your head, even if it's every day. He's your attorney – he should be available to talk when it's convenient for you, not him, right?**

Well, yes and no. While you have every right to expect reasonable and customary updates from your attorney as your case progresses, you should respect your lawyer's professional time and schedule, and not abuse it with incessant calls to the office every time you have "just one more question." In this regard, most attorneys will discuss the preferred means of communication with them at the outset of the relationship, so that you know what to expect. Be respectful of your lawyer's office policies in this regard, and always be courteous to the lawyer's staff. It is the polite thing to do, and the right thing to do, in order to keep your relationship sound and in good working order.

Many lawyers appreciate the opportunity to respond via email. That way, they have a record of your inquiry, you have a record of their response, and both sides can communicate when their schedules reasonably permit.

2. **Run everything your lawyer tells you by every friend and relative you know who's ever been represented by a lawyer in an accident, and ask for their opinions. They'll tell you if your lawyer is "on track," right? After all, two or three heads are better than one, aren't they? And if their advice differs from your lawyer's, call your lawyer right away and demand to know why he thinks differently!**

Actually, no. If you've been reasonably careful in hiring an attorney who is knowledgeable and well respected, then your best option is to respect that lawyer's advice with regard to your case, and not second guess it by "running it by" others who simply don't have the formal legal training, experience, or thorough knowledge of the facts of your case that your lawyer has. Remember, no matter what you may think, your case is not "just like" anyone else's. Take your legal advice from *your* lawyer, not from someone else's lawyer or a friend who happens to have a law degree.

3. **Discuss your case with anyone and everyone who will listen. That way, the facts will stay fresh in your mind and you may pick up some good ideas to pass on to your lawyer.**

Actually, no. A good attorney will always advise you not to discuss the facts of your case with anyone, and there is a reason. If and when you have your deposition taken, one of the questions that a good insurance defense lawyer is bound to ask is "who have you discussed your case with?" Every one of those persons might then be subpoenaed to have their own depositions taken, and they will be queried about anything and everything you told them about your accident. So do yourself a favor. Discuss your case with your attorney, and no one else. Those conversations are subject to the "attorney-client privilege," but other conversations are not similarly protected. And if you think your attorney will benefit from your non-lawyer friends' advice, you are likely mistaken. Look at it this way. Would you pass on your friends' advice to your doctor about how best to perform an upcoming operation?

There is something else to keep in mind here. As the client, you own the attorney-client privilege of confidentiality. If you disclose to friends and family members your private conversations with your attorney, you most likely have just waived your attorney-client privilege as to those conversations, forever. Don't do it. If friends ask if your lawyer thinks you have a good case, tell them that you really cannot discuss the case, or your lawyer's communications with you. They should understand.

4. **If something you did may have helped cause the accident, shhhhhhhh, don't tell the lawyer. It will only distract him or her from getting you a large settlement. After all, if your lawyer doesn't know, the other side probably won't find out either right?**

Actually, no. Because everything you communicate with your attorney is strictly confidential, one of the worst things you can do is withhold important information from your attorney about your case, period. Your lawyer is on your side, remember? Do *not* hamper his or her ability to effectively represent you by withholding information. Err on the side of inclusion, and let your attorney decide what is important and what isn't. That is an important part of their responsibility, and is essential if they are to be effective in representing you.

5. **Exaggerate your injuries and their effects on your daily life so your claim might be worth more. Who's to know otherwise?**

The insurance company for the other driver, that's who. These companies frequently hire private investigators to investigate the extent to which injuries actually affect the daily activities of lawsuit plaintiffs. If you exaggerate these effects, you do a tremendous disservice to your attorney, yourself, and ultimately your case. Don't even think about it. It is essential that you be completely honest and forthright with your lawyer at all times. That one key piece of information you withhold could be a ticking bomb that will blow your case to pieces.

6. **Don't bother with medical treatment follow up or all those unnecessary tests that the doctors want you to**

have. They're a waste of time – you know your own body, right?

Cyclists are often seasoned athletes, and have an acute awareness of their own bodies and how they respond to injuries and the healing process. Sometimes, athletes prefer to manage their own therapy and treatment, believing they know better than the trained medical professionals. If you wish to manage your own recovery, that is certainly your prerogative. But if you do, be mindful of the fact that when evaluating accident claims, adjusters frequently and carefully examine the history and schedule of medical treatment obtained by the injured party. If there are significant "gaps" in treatment, that can have a significant adverse effect upon the plaintiff's credibility, and ultimately the value of your claim.

The most common scenario here is when an injured cyclist is prescribed physical therapy. He or she may attend a session or two, and then cancel future appointments, believing the exercises are simple enough and can just be performed at home. Months later, when their condition deteriorates and they are feeling worse instead of better, they re-initiate physical therapy. Unfortunately, if there is a substantial gap in treatment, they may not be able to recover the expense of that subsequent treatment, because the adjuster will question its necessity or its relationship to the accident that preceded it. In my opinion, if you are prescribed physical therapy to help the healing process, it is always best to complete the course of treatment diligently, from start to finish. Follow your doctor's recommended course of treatment. In the long run, you will be glad you did.

CHAPTER 18

AUTO INSURANCE CHECKUP: IMPORTANT THINGS TO KNOW

I am not an insurance agent, and have no insurance to sell you. I have nothing to gain by your decisions about how much coverage to have, or where to purchase it. Nevertheless, as someone who represents and cares about cyclists, I do have an interest in educating you about certain types of coverage that all riders should have if they are serious about protecting themselves and their families.

If you've already been in an accident, then this advice may be coming a little too late. On the other hand, if you haven't, it's time for an auto insurance checkup.

Auto insurance? What does that have to do with me getting hurt on my bike?

The answer is, plenty. If you are badly hurt in a crash, it is often the case that the person who hit you may not have sufficient liability insurance to adequately compensate you. Where I live in Northern Virginia and in the DC area generally, statistics show that more and more drivers are out there on the road with *insufficient* coverage, or *no coverage at all.*[21]

That's the bad news. The good news is that you don't have to be a victim in that circumstance. By having sufficient UM/UIM (uninsured – underinsured motorist coverage) on your *auto* policy, you can tap in to your own insurance even if you are on your bicycle and are hit by a third party.

Most folks don't know if they have UM/UIM coverage or not. To find out, pull out your policy, and read the "declaration page" on the front. If you have UM/UIM coverage, it will be listed next to the dollar limits on your liability and property damage coverages. If you are still unsure, call up your insurance agent today to review your coverage. The chances are, that you have too little insurance. And if you're thinking, "I can't afford it," consider this: can you afford devastating health care bills that could wipe out your life savings and bankrupt you and your family?

Consider the following:

- Most riders have way too little auto insurance. They pride themselves in safe riding practices, and are doing everything else they know of to protect themselves.

[21] A 2011 insurance industry survey confirmed that on average throughout the United States, one in seven motorists is driving with no insurance coverage at all. http://www.insurance-research.org/research-publications/uninsured-motorists-2011-edition-march-2011

- Bike accidents produce far worse injuries than car accidents. (As if you didn't know.)

- According to recent studies funded by the insurance industry, the number of uninsured motorists nationally is climbing, and exceeds 20% in some states. That means *one* in *five* motorists are completely uninsured. That's right. In many states *one in five* drivers is completely without coverage of any kind.

- What happens if you are seriously injured and are permanently disabled as a result of carelessness by an uninsured driver? What happens if you suffer serious injuries that preclude you from working? Serious injuries that could require medical services that far exceed your health care benefits, resulting in a financial catastrophe for you and your family? Answer: NO INSURANCE MONEY AVAILABLE TO PAY YOUR CLAIM.

- If this happens, you're in a world of financial hurt brother – a world of hurt that could have been prevented if you had a big, fat "UM"/"UIM" (uninsured/underinsured motorist) "rider" (no pun intended) on your policy. With that UM/UIM coverage, you never have to worry again about whether that careless knucklehead who injured you has coverage, because YOU have it regardless. If you are injured by a careless driver who has too little coverage or no coverage at all, your UM/UIM "rider" on your policy kicks into gear and is there as a source of funds available for recovery to compensate you for your losses. Is it expensive? No!!! Dollar for dollar, it's one of the biggest bangs for the insurance buck you can get, and insurance companies in Virginia *have* to make it available by law. Would they do it otherwise? In my opinion, probably not, which is why the chances are, your trusty insurance agent never even suggested it when he sold you the policy, and even worse, may even try to talk you out of buying it. Don't accept that. You're a target out there, remember? Get the most UIM coverage you can afford. As a cyclist, you cannot afford not to.

Now let me say a few words about "bicycle insurance" policies that are now being offered. For those of you who are cycling purists and who don't own a car, there are bike-specific policies available to help you minimize your exposure in a number of respects. Many of these insurance products are excellent, but it is important to understand their limitations as well.

First, let me summarize the good points. Most bicycle insurance policies are well tailored to adequately address property damages to your high-end bicycle if you are in a bad crash. Unlike many auto or homeowner's insurance adjusters, insurance professionals who handle claims under bicycle policies have a thorough understanding of bicycle values and replacement costs, and you are usually well positioned to be adequately compensated for your property damages.

In addition to property damages, some bicycle insurance policies have coverage for medical bill payments – sometimes up to $100,000. While this may sound adequate, however, it may well not be if you are badly injured. It is also important to understand that these policies only cover medical bills. They don't pay a dime for your lost wages attributable to time away from work, the cost of future medical care if you need it, and most importantly, they don't compensate you for the pain and suffering you experienced from being injured. They pay your medical bills, and that's all. It may be better than nothing, but for most of my clients, it is not enough to adequately compensate them for their losses.

I AM NOT AN INSURANCE AGENT. TO LEARN MORE, CONTACT A QUALIFIED INSURANCE AGENT IN YOUR STATE FOR ALL THE INFORMATION YOU NEED TO OBTAIN SUFFICIENT COVERAGE. DO IT TODAY! PROTECT YOURSELF!

CHAPTER 19

THE OTHER DRIVER'S LIABILITY INSURANCE – WHAT'S THE BIG DEAL?

If the other driver doesn't have liability insurance coverage, and you didn't have the wisdom to take out "UIM coverage" on your own policy, then recovering compensation for your injuries may be extremely difficult. In order to understand why, you need to understand what the legal process can and cannot do for you as the victim of someone else's negligence.

Regardless of whether the other driver has liability coverage, you still have the right to file a lawsuit against that person for negligence. If you win your case at trial, the court will "enter" what is known as a "judgment," ordering that person to pay you a sum of money. What many people fail to understand, however, is that there is no guarantee you will ever be paid that money, because it doesn't come from the court, it comes from the defendant. If the defendant simply doesn't have it (either by way of cash, real estate, investments, or other assets that can be converted to cash), you may be flat out of luck.

Procedures vary by state, but the law does permit you to discover what assets the defendant has, and where they are located. Generally, this is done by serving the defendant (now called the "judgment debtor") with "debtor's interrogatories," which are questions that have to be responded to fully, in writing, and under oath. If the defendant refuses, the judge may find him in "contempt of court," and could even put him in jail for that contempt until he complies.

Navigating these legal procedures can be legally and procedurally complex, and is best handled by your attorney. However, most personal injury attorneys I know make it clear in their fee agreements that the contingent fee covers only taking the case to trial. It does not cover "post-judgment" work involving attempts to collect on the judgment. Typically, you must pay your attorney their hourly fee for that, with no guarantee of a return on that investment.

If assets can be located (say a boat, investments, a piece of real estate, or a bank account somewhere), you can employ the jurisdiction and authority of the court to "levy" on your judgment, and "attach" (a nice legal term for *take or freeze*) those assets in order to satisfy your judgment. Depending upon state laws, this "right of attachment" may include garnishing (another nice legal tern for *taking*) the defendant's wages to the tune of a specified percentage per pay-period until the judgment is satisfied. The challenge here, of course, is that if the judgment is large and the person's salary small, that person may well just file for bankruptcy in order to get out from under it. Once again, you may be flat out of luck.

All of this comes down to the fact that if insurance is available, you need to find out about it because collecting your judgment from the negligent driver's personal assets simply may not be feasible. By this I mean that, even in cases where the defendant does not have a liability policy on the vehicle they were driving at the time, there may be coverage under a spouse's policy, or even some other family member in the same household, that could be applicable to provide coverage in your case. This is where the experience of a qualified lawyer can be extremely valuable. Your attorney should know what questions to ask and otherwise how to identify each and every possible source of insurance coverage available in a case.

Similarly, if the negligent party was doing an errand for his or her boss or otherwise performing a work function when he or she was driving at the time of the accident, or if that driver was driving a work vehicle, the employer's commercial liability policy could be available to provide coverage. This is an extremely important fact to find out, as commercial policies tend to have *much higher levels of coverage* than personal policies, which could be extremely helpful if your injuries are severe. Once again, an experienced personal injury attorney will find out all relevant facts that may uncover these available sources of coverage through the "discovery" process. [For more on "discovery," see Chapter 15].

CHAPTER 20

INSURANCE SUBROGATION

(WHAT YOU DON'T KNOW CAN COST YOU $$THOUSANDS)

If you've been injured in an accident, and you have used your health insurance to pay for treating your injuries, it is important that you know about "subrogation." Just like the doctrine of "contributory negligence," "subrogation" is a scary sounding legal principle that is extremely important to know about.

I am always amazed at how significantly this can affect the client's rights, and how few attorneys have a thorough knowledge of how it works. While the details can be extremely complex, in a nutshell, it works like this.

In the hours and months following your accident, you submit your medical treatment bills to your health insurance provider, who processes them in the normal course. During this period, you may or may not have yet hired an attorney to assist you, and if you have hired a lawyer, the process of pursuing your claim may only be in its beginning stages.

Then, one day in the mail, a letter arrives, often from a firm other than your health insurer, who tells you that they "represent" your health insurer as a "subrogation agent," and need some detailed information about your "accident." While some health insurance companies have internal subrogation divisions that handle this, most of them contract it out to third party entities that serve essentially as subrogation "collection agents" for your health insurer. Typically, they send you some forms asking for some details about your accident, including the date, time and circumstances, the nature of your injuries, the name and address of your lawyer if you have one, and where you received treatment. More often than not, these letters are quite forceful in tone, and make it clear that they have a right to the information and they demand that it be sent promptly. In some cases, particularly if you delay in responding, the letters even contain threatening language telling you that if you don't provide all of the information requested immediately, your health insurance benefits could be reduced or even cut off entirely.

Wow!! Are you kidding? How can they do that? And what do they want with this information?

If you receive a letter like this, the chances are that buried deep in the fine print of your health insurance policy is a "subrogation provision," which says that if you receive money from a negligent party who caused your accident (either by way of a negotiated settlement or by way of a jury award in court), the health insurance company gets to be <u>paid back out of that money</u> all of the benefits that it paid out for your accident-related medical treatment. That's right. The benefits they paid out to the hospital and your doctors were just a loan.

But isn't that money for me to compensate me for my injuries? I've paid my health insurance premiums. How come the insurance company gets to take that compensation money back from me??

Well, the answer, believe it or not, is that legally, *you* agreed to *let* them. That's right. By taking out that policy of insurance, you entered into a form of legal contract with that health insurance provider, and the subrogation clause is one of the many terms of that contract. If you are like many people, you probably haven't read all of the fine print in your policy, which is why you probably weren't aware of subrogation.

But that isn't fair!! How do they get to do this?? What did I pay my premiums for if I have to pay back my benefits?

Well, some states agree with that point of view, and have passed "anti-subrogation" laws that make this kind of contract provision illegal and unenforceable. Virginia is such a state, and the statute says that if health insurers wish to provide coverage in Virginia, they cannot have enforceable subrogation rights.[22]

Whew!! So if I'm in Virginia (or another state that has an "anti-subrogation law"), I'm safe from this practice, right?

[22] See Va. Code § 38.2-3405.

Well, no. Unfortunately, the U.S. Supreme Court has ruled that some types of "self-funded" health care plans can still maintain enforceable subrogation rights even in states like Virginia that have "anti-subrogation" statutes. This is because certain so-called "self-funded" health care "plans" fall under the regulatory jurisdiction of a federal statute known as "ERISA" (otherwise known as the Employee Retirement Income Security Act). If your health care plan is an "ERISA" plan, then it comes under exclusive federal jurisdiction, and is not subject to any state's "anti-subrogation" protection.

Well, if I have one of these ERISA plans, does it that mean I really have to pay everything back?

Not necessarily! Many health insurance carriers will authorize their subrogation "agents" to negotiate with you (or, preferably, your attorney, who is well versed in the details of subrogation) over how much of your settlement (or jury award) you have to pay back to them. In many cases, they may be willing to settle for significantly less than 100% of the benefits paid out.

When and how to negotiate with these collection agents is a tricky business, and requires a thorough knowledge of the applicable laws, regulations, and the specific terms of your policy. In most cases, it is best left to your attorney. Some lawyers (including me, by the way) will include this service as part of their representation of you on your claim. Others, as a matter of policy, specifically indicate in their fee agreements that this is an entirely separate matter, for which they want additional compensation (either by way of an hourly fee for time spent on it, or by way of a slightly higher percentage of your recovery if they are representing you on a "contingent fee" basis).

Obviously, whether this additional compensation is warranted depends on a number of factors, including the size of the subrogation claim, how hard your carrier is pursuing their subrogation rights against you, and of course, the amount of additional compensation requested by your attorney (if any). As a general proposition, however, you should discuss any communications to and from a subrogation agent with your lawyer before responding to any request for information about your accident from anyone, including a "subrogation agent" claiming to represent your health insurance carrier.

Why is that so important?

Because quite often, subrogation agents will insist that their carriers have rock solid subrogation rights that they really don't have, or may not have. I have had numerous experiences in which, in response to these threatening letters, I have written to these "agents" and demanded to see all of the necessary documentation to prove that they were legally entitled to the money they were demanding. After a few spirited exchanges in which they failed to provide the necessary documents, they simply disappeared and stopped making demands on my clients.

What does that tell you about the validity of these claims? In my opinion, it tells us that some claims may be valid, and some are not, and it's important to know the answer *before* agreeing to pay these people one red cent of your settlement or judgment proceeds. Just because they *say* they are entitled to it does not mean that they really are. If a company's subrogation claim is legitimate, their agents will be more than happy to provide your lawyer with the complete policy, including the contractual language they are relying upon to support their claim.

NEVER ASSUME THAT THESE COMPANIES HAVE SOLID LEGAL CLAIMS ON YOUR SETTLEMENT OR JURY PROCEEDS UNTIL THEY CAN PROVE THEIR ENTITLEMENT TO THOSE CLAIMS WITH THOROUGH, COMPLETE DOCUMENTATION.

Let's be clear here. I am NOT suggesting that these companies' letters should be ignored. That unwise course of action could, under some circumstances, lead to the cancellation of your health coverage. What I AM suggesting is that you respond carefully and appropriately to these aggressive tactics, preferably under the guidance of someone who understands the numerous complexities and subtleties of this confusing realm.

APPENDICES 1

BICYCLE LAWS IN VIRGINIA, DC AND MARYLAND

Set out below are some state, county and city codes in the Washington, DC area concerning bicycles that are in effect as of this book's date of publication. I include them here for your reference, and to aid your understanding of how these laws are structured, and how they govern bicycle riding on public roads. For the sake of brevity, some of the code provisions are edited to include only those portions of the laws that apply to bicycles.

In reviewing these laws, however, please be mindful of the following important points:

- These are state statutes, county code provisions and city / municipal regulations only. Much of the law governing the rights and responsibilities of cyclists can also be found in published court opinions, otherwise known as "case law" or "common law." Researching and interpreting case law is best left to qualified attorneys.

- Bicycle laws are continually enacted, amended, and even abolished. Do not assume that the laws on these pages are current when you read them, even though they were on the date of publication. While the provisions set forth in these appendices may be a helpful starting point for you, you should always research their current status to make sure they are still in effect, or have not been changed in a material way that could affect your case.

- Nothing in this appendix should be considered to be legal advice. Like anything else that requires experience and training, there is no substitute for a competent lawyer's advice on the current status of the law in your jurisdiction.

APPENDIX 1

THE COMMONWEALTH OF VIRGINIA (STATUTES)

TITLE 46.2. MOTOR VEHICLES
SUBTITLE III. OPERATION
CHAPTER 8. REGULATION OF TRAFFIC

I. Article 12. Bicycles

Va. Code Ann. § 46.2-903 (2013). Riding or driving vehicles other than bicycles, electric power-assisted bicycles, or electric personal assistive mobility devices on sidewalks

No person shall ride or drive any vehicle other than (i) an emergency vehicle, as defined in § 46.2-920, (ii) a vehicle engaged in snow or ice removal and control operations, (iii) a wheel chair or wheel chair conveyance, whether self-propelled or otherwise, (iv) a bicycle, (v) an electric personal assistive mobility device, or (vi) an electric power-assisted bicycle on the sidewalks of any county, city, or town of the Commonwealth.

Va. Code Ann. § 46.2-904 (2013). Use of roller skates and skateboards on sidewalks and shared-use paths; operation of bicycles, motorized skateboards or foot-scooters, motor-driven cycles, electric power-assisted bicycles, and electric personal assistive mobility devices on sidewalks and crosswalks and shared-use paths; local ordinances

The governing body of any county, city, or town may by ordinance prohibit the use of roller skates and skateboards and / or the riding of bicycles, electric personal assistive mobility devices, motorized skateboards or foot-scooters, motor-driven cycles, or electric power-assisted bicycles on designated sidewalks or crosswalks, including those of any church, school, recreational facility, or any business property open to the public where such activity is prohibited. Signs indicating such prohibition shall be conspicuously posted in general areas where use of roller skates and skateboards, and / or bicycle, electric personal assistive mobility devices, motorized skateboards or foot-scooters, motor-driven cycles, or electric power-assisted bicycle riding is prohibited.

A person riding a bicycle, electric personal assistive mobility device, motorized skateboard or foot-scooter, motor-driven cycle, or an electric power-assisted bicycle on a sidewalk, shared-use path, or across a roadway on a crosswalk, shall yield the right-of-way to any pedestrian and shall give an audible signal before overtaking and passing any pedestrian.

No person shall ride a bicycle, electric personal assistive mobility device, motorized skateboard or foot-scooter, motor-driven cycle, or an electric power-assisted bicycle on a sidewalk, or across a roadway on a crosswalk, where such use of bicycles, electric personal assistive mobility devices, motorized skateboards or foot-scooters, motor-driven cycles, or electric power-assisted bicycles is prohibited by official traffic control devices.

A person riding a bicycle, electric personal assistive mobility device, motorized skateboard or foot-scooter, motor-driven cycle, or an electric power-assisted bicycle on a sidewalk, shared-use path, or across a roadway on a crosswalk, shall have all the rights and duties of a pedestrian under the same circumstances.

A violation of any ordinance adopted pursuant to this section shall be punishable by a civil penalty of not more than $50.

Va. Code Ann. § 46.2-905 (2013). Riding bicycles, electric personal assistive mobility devices, electric power-assisted bicycles, motor-driven cycles, and mopeds on roadways and bicycle paths

Any person operating a bicycle, electric personal assistive mobility device, electric power-assisted bicycle, or moped on a roadway at less than the normal speed of traffic at the time and place under conditions then existing shall ride as close as safely practicable to the right curb or edge of the roadway, except under any of the following circumstances:

1. When overtaking and passing another vehicle proceeding in the same direction;

2. When preparing for a left turn at an intersection or into a private road or driveway;

3. When reasonably necessary to avoid conditions including, but not limited to, fixed or moving objects, parked or moving vehicles, pedestrians, animals, surface hazards, or sub-

standard width lanes that make it unsafe to continue along the right curb or edge;

4. When avoiding riding in a lane that must turn or diverge to the right; and

5. When riding upon a one-way road or highway, a person may also ride as near the left-hand curb or edge of such roadway as safely practicable.

For purposes of this section, a "substandard width lane" is a lane too narrow for a bicycle, electric personal assistive mobility device, electric power-assisted bicycle, motorized skateboard or foot-scooter, or moped and another vehicle to pass safely side by side within the lane.

Persons riding bicycles, electric personal assistive mobility devices, or electric power-assisted bicycles on a highway shall not ride more than two abreast. Persons riding two abreast shall not impede the normal and reasonable movement of traffic, shall move into a single file formation as quickly as is practicable when being overtaken from the rear by a faster moving vehicle, and, on a laned roadway, shall ride in a single lane.

Notwithstanding any other provision of law to the contrary, the Department of Conservation and Recreation shall permit the operation of electric personal assistive mobility devices on any bicycle path or trail designated by the Department for such use.

Va. Code Ann. § 46.2-906 (2013). Carrying articles or passengers on bicycles, electric personal assistive mobility devices, electric power-assisted bicycles, and mopeds

No person operating a bicycle, electric personal assistive mobility device, electric power-assisted bicycle, or moped on a highway shall carry any package, bundle, or article that prevents the driver from keeping at least one hand on the handlebars.

No bicycle or moped shall be used to carry more persons at one time than the number of persons for which it was designed or is equipped, except that an adult bicycle rider may carry a child less than six years old if such child is securely attached to the bicycle in a seat or trailer designed for carrying children.

Va. Code Ann. § 46.2-906.1 (2013). Local ordinances may require riders of bicycles, electric personal assistive mobility devices, and electric power-assisted bicycles to wear helmets

The governing body of any county, city or town may, by ordinance, provide that every person 14 years of age or younger shall wear a protective helmet that at least meets the Consumer Product Safety Commission standard whenever riding or being carried on a bicycle, an electric personal assistive mobility device, a toy vehicle, or an electric power-assisted bicycle on any highway as defined in § 46.2-100, sidewalk, or public bicycle path.

Violation of any such ordinance shall be punishable by a fine of $25. However, such fine shall be suspended (i) for first-time violators and (ii) for violators who, subsequent to the violation but prior to imposition of the fine, purchase helmets of the type required by the ordinance.

Violation of any such ordinance shall not constitute negligence, or assumption of risk, be considered in mitigation of damages of whatever nature, be admissible in evidence, or be the subject of comment by counsel in any action for the recovery of damages arising out of the operation of any bicycle, electric personal assistive mobility device, toy vehicle, or electric power-assisted bicycle, nor shall anything in this section change any existing law, rule, or procedure pertaining to any civil action.

Va. Code Ann. § 46.2-907 (2013). Overtaking and passing vehicles

A person riding a bicycle, electric personal assistive mobility device, electric power-assisted bicycle, motorized skateboard or foot-scooter, or moped may overtake and pass another vehicle on either the left or right side, staying in the same lane as the overtaken vehicle, or changing to a different lane, or riding off the roadway as necessary to pass with safety.

A person riding a bicycle, electric personal assistive mobility device, electric power-assisted bicycle, motorized skateboard or foot-scooter, or moped may overtake and pass another vehicle only under conditions that permit the movement to be made with safety.

A person riding a bicycle, electric personal assistive mobility device, electric power-assisted bicycle, motorized skateboard or foot-scooter, or moped shall not travel between two lanes of traffic moving in the same direction, except where one lane is a separate turn lane or a mandatory turn lane.

Except as otherwise provided in this section, a person riding a bicycle, electric personal assistive mobility device, electric power-assisted bicycle, motorized skateboard or foot-scooter, or moped shall comply with all rules applicable to the driver of a motor vehicle when overtaking and passing.

Va. Code Ann. § 46.2-908 (2013). Registration of bicycle, electric personal assistive mobility device, and electric power-assisted bicycle serial numbers

Any person who owns a bicycle, electric personal assistive mobility device, or electric power-assisted bicycle may register its serial number with the local law-enforcement agency of the political subdivision in which such person resides.

II. Articles 3-7. Traffic Signs; Passing; Turning; Signals; Reckless & Improper Driving

Va. Code Ann. § 46.2-833 (2013). Traffic lights; penalty

B. Notwithstanding any other provision of law, if a driver of a motorcycle or moped or a bicycle rider approaches an intersection that is controlled by a traffic light, the driver or rider may proceed through the intersection on a steady red light only if the driver or rider (i) comes to a full and complete stop at the intersection for two complete cycles of the traffic light or for two minutes, whichever is shorter, (ii) exercises due care as provided by law, (iii) otherwise treats the traffic control device as a stop sign, (iv) determines that it is safe to proceed, and (v) yields the right of way to the driver of any vehicle approaching on such other highway from either direction.

Violation of any provision of this section shall constitute a traffic infraction punishable by a fine of no more than $350.

Va. Code Ann. § 46.2-839 (2013). Passing bicycle, electric personal assistive mobility device, electric power-assisted bicycle, moped, animal, or animal-drawn vehicle

Any driver of any vehicle overtaking a bicycle, electric personal assistive mobility device, electric power-assisted bicycle, moped, animal, or animal-drawn vehicle proceeding in the same direction shall pass at a reasonable speed at least two feet to the left of the overtaken bicycle, electric personal assistive mobility device, electric power-assisted bicycle, moped, animal, or animal-drawn vehicle and shall not again proceed to the right side of the highway until safely clear of such overtaken bicycle, electric personal assistive mobility device, electric power-assisted bicycle, moped, animal, or animal-drawn vehicle.

Va. Code Ann. § 46.2-847 (2013). Left turns by bicycles, electric personal assistive mobility devices, electric power-assisted bicycles, and mopeds

A person riding a bicycle, electric personal assistive mobility device, electric power-assisted bicycle, or moped and intending to turn left shall either follow a course described in § 46.2-846[23] or make the turn as provided in this section.

[23] Va. Code Ann. § 46.2-846(A) (2013). Required position and method of turning at intersections

1. Right turns: Both the approach for a right turn and a right turn shall be made as close as practicable to the right curb or edge of the roadway.
2. Left turns on two-way roadways: At any intersection where traffic is permitted to move in both directions on each roadway entering the intersection, an approach for a left turn shall be made from the right half of the roadway and as close as possible to the roadway's center line, passing to the right of the center line where it enters the intersection. After entering the intersection, the left turn shall be made so as to leave the intersection to the right of the center line of the roadway being entered. Whenever practicable, the left turn shall be made to the left of the center of the intersection.
3. Left turns on other than two-way roadways: At any intersection where traffic is restricted to one direction on one or more of the roadways, and at any crossover from one roadway of a divided highway to another roadway thereof on which traffic moves in the opposite direction, the driver intending to turn left at any such intersection or crossover shall approach the intersection or crossover in the extreme left lane lawfully available to traffic moving in the direction of travel of such vehicle and after entering the intersection or crossover the left turn shall be made so as to leave the intersection or crossover, as nearly as practicable, in the left lane lawfully available to traffic moving in such direction upon the roadway being entered.

A person riding a bicycle, electric personal assistive mobility device, electric power-assisted bicycle, or moped and intending to turn left shall approach the turn as close as practicable to the right curb or edge of the roadway. After proceeding across the intersecting roadway, the rider shall comply with traffic signs or signals and continue his turn as close as practicable to the right curb or edge of the roadway being entered.

Notwithstanding the foregoing provisions of this section, the Commissioner of Highways and local authorities, in their respective jurisdictions, may cause official traffic control devices to be placed at intersections to direct that a specific course be traveled by turning bicycles, electric personal assistive mobility devices, electric power-assisted bicycles, and mopeds. When such devices are so placed, no person shall turn a bicycle, electric personal assistive mobility device, electric power-assisted bicycle, or moped other than as directed by such devices.

Va. Code Ann. § 46.2-849 (2013). How signals given

A. Signals required by § 46.2-848[24] shall be given by means of the hand and arm or by some mechanical or electrical device approved by the Superintendent, in the manner specified in this section. Whenever the signal is given by means of the

[24] Va. Code Ann. § 46.2-848 (2013). Signals required on backing, stopping, or turning Every driver who intends to back, stop, turn, or partly turn from a direct line shall first see that such movement can be made safely and, whenever the operation of any other vehicle may be affected by such movement, shall give the signals required in this article, plainly visible to the driver of such other vehicle, of his intention to make such movement.

hand and arm, the driver shall indicate his intention to start, stop, turn, or partly turn by extending the hand and arm beyond the left side of the vehicle in the manner following:

1. For left turn or to pull to the left, the arm shall be extended in a horizontal position straight from and level with the shoulder;

2. For right turn or to pull to the right, the arm shall be extended upward;

3. For slowing down or stopping, the arm shall be extended downward.

B. Wherever the lawful speed is more than 35 miles per hour, such signals shall be given continuously for a distance of at least 100 feet, and in all other cases at least 50 feet, before slowing down, stopping, turning, or partly turning.

C. A person riding a bicycle, electric personal assistive mobility device, electric power-assisted bicycle, or moped shall signal his intention to stop or turn. Such signals, however, need not be given continuously if both hands are needed in the control or operation of the bicycle, electric personal assistive mobility device, electric power-assisted bicycle, or moped.

D. Notwithstanding the foregoing provisions of this section, a person operating a bicycle, electric personal assistive mobility device, electric power-assisted bicycle, or moped may signal a right turn or pull to the right by extending the right hand and arm in a horizontal position straight from and level with the shoulder beyond the right side of the bicycle, electric personal assistive mobility device, electric power-assisted bicycle, or moped, and may signal slowing down or stopping by extending the right arm downward.

Va. Code Ann. § 46.2-856 (2013). Passing two vehicles abreast

A person shall be guilty of reckless driving who passes or attempts to pass two other vehicles abreast, moving in the same direction, except on highways having separate roadways of three or more lanes for each direction of travel, or on designated one-way streets or highways. This section shall not apply, however, to a motor vehicle passing two other vehicles when one or both of such other vehicles is a bicycle, electric personal assistive mobility device, electric power-assisted bicycle, or moped; nor shall this section apply to a bicycle, electric personal assistive mobility device, electric power-assisted bicycle, or moped passing two other vehicles.

Va. Code Ann. § 46.2-857 (2013). Driving two abreast in a single lane

A person shall be guilty of reckless driving who drives any motor vehicle so as to be abreast of another vehicle in a lane designed for one vehicle, or drives any motor vehicle so as to travel abreast of any other vehicle traveling in a lane designed for one vehicle. . . . [T]his section shall not apply to . . . (ii) a motor vehicle traveling in the same lane of traffic as a bicycle, electric personal assistive mobility device, electric power-assisted bicycle, or moped. . . .

III. Miscellaneous

Va. Code Ann. § 46.2-800 (2013). Riding bicycles, electric personal assistive mobility devices, electric power-assisted bicycles, or mopeds; riding or driving animals

Every person riding a bicycle, electric personal assistive mobility device, electric power-assisted bicycle, moped, or an animal or driving an animal on a highway shall be subject to the provisions of this chapter and shall have all of the rights and duties applicable to the driver of a vehicle, unless the context of the provision clearly indicates otherwise.

The provisions of subsections A and C of § 46.2-920 applicable to operation of emergency vehicles under emergency conditions shall also apply, mutatis mutandis, to bicycles, electric personal assistive mobility devices, electric power-assisted bicycles, and mopeds operated under similar emergency conditions by law-enforcement officers.

Va. Code Ann. § 46.2-808 (2013). Commonwealth Transportation Board may prohibit certain uses of controlled access highways; penalty

A. The Commonwealth Transportation Board may, when necessary to promote safety, prohibit the use of controlled access highways or any part thereof by any or all of the following:

2. Persons riding bicycles, electric power-assisted bicycles,

electric personal assistive mobility devices, or mopeds. . . .

B. The termini of any section of controlled access highways, use of which is restricted under the provisions of this section, shall be clearly indicated by a conspicuous marker.

C. This section shall not apply to any vehicle or equipment owned or controlled by the Virginia Department of Transportation, while actually engaged in the construction, reconstruction, or maintenance of highways or to any vehicle or equipment for which a permit has been obtained for operation on such highway.

Any person violating a restriction or prohibition imposed pursuant to this section shall be guilty of a traffic infraction.

Va. Code. Ann. § 46.2-908.1 (2013). Electric personal assistive mobility devices, electrically powered toy vehicles, and electric power-assisted bicycles

. . . Nothing in this section shall prohibit the operation of an electric personal assistive mobility device or motorized skateboard or foot-scooter in the crosswalk of any highway where the use of such crosswalk is authorized for pedestrians, bicycles, or electric power-assisted bicycles.

Operation of . . . bicycles and electric power-assisted bicycles is prohibited on any Interstate Highway System component except as provided by the section.

The Commonwealth Transportation Board may authorize the

use of bicycles on an Interstate Highway System Component provided the operation is limited to bicycle or pedestrian facilities that are barrier separated from the roadway and automobile traffic and such component meets all applicable safety requirements established by federal and state law.

Va. Code. Ann. § 46.2-932 (2013). Playing on highways; use of toy vehicle on highways, persons riding bicycles, electric personal assistive mobility devices, electric power-assisted bicycles, mopeds, etc., not to attach to vehicles; exception

A. No person shall play on a highway, other than on the sidewalks thereof, within a city or town or on any part of a highway outside the limits of a city or town designated by the Commissioner of Highways exclusively for vehicular travel. No person shall use any toy vehicle on the roadway of any highway that (i) has a speed limit greater than 25 miles per hour, (ii) has more than two travel lanes, or (iii) is located outside a residence district as defined in § 46.2-100. The governing bodies of counties, cities, and towns may designate areas on highways under their control where play is permitted and may impose reasonable restrictions on play on such highways. Persons using such devices, except bicycles, electric personal assistive mobility devices, electric power-assisted bicycles, mopeds, and motorcycles, shall keep as near as safely practicable to the far right side or edge of the right traffic lane so that they will be proceeding in the same direction as other traffic.

No person riding on any bicycle, electric personal assistive mobility device, electric power-assisted bicycle, moped, roller skates, skateboards or other devices on wheels or runners, shall attach the same or himself to any vehicle on a highway.

B. Notwithstanding the provisions of subsection A of this section, the governing body of Arlington County may by ordinance permit the use of devices on wheels or runners on highways under such county's control, subject to such limitations and conditions as the governing body may deem necessary and reasonable.

TITLE 46.2. MOTOR VEHICLES (cont'd)
SUBTITLE III. OPERATION (cont'd)
CHAPTER 10. MOTOR VEHICLE & EQUIPMENT SAFETY

Va. Code Ann. § 46.2-1015 (2013). Lights on bicycles, electric personal assistive mobility devices, electric power-assisted bicycles, and mopeds

A. Every bicycle, electric personal assistive mobility device, electric power-assisted bicycle, and moped when in use between sunset and sunrise shall be equipped with a headlight on the front emitting a white light visible in clear weather from a distance of at least 500 feet to the front and a red reflector visible from a distance of at least 600 feet to the rear when directly in front of lawful lower beams of headlights on a motor vehicle. Such lights and reflector shall be of types approved by the Superintendent.

In addition to the foregoing provisions of this section, a bicycle or its rider may be equipped with lights or reflectors. These lights may be steady burning or blinking.

B. Every bicycle, or its rider, shall be equipped with a taillight on the rear emitting a red light plainly visible in clear weather from a distance of at least 500 feet to the rear when in use between sunset and sunrise and operating on any highway with a speed limit of 35 mph or greater. Any such taillight shall be of a type approved by the Superintendent.

Va. Code Ann. § 46.2-1025 (2013). Flashing amber, purple, or green warning lights

A. The following vehicles may be equipped with flashing, blinking, or alternating amber warning lights of types approved by the Superintendent:

17. Vehicles used to lead or provide escorts for bicycle races authorized by the Department of Transportation or the locality in which the race is being conducted . . .

Va. Code Ann. § 46.2-1051 (2013). Certain local governments may impose restrictions on operations of certain vehicles

The governing body of any county, city, or town which is located within the Northern Virginia Planning District may provide by ordinance that no person shall operate and no owner shall permit the operation of, either on a highway or on public or private property within 500 feet of any residential district, any . . . electric power-assisted bicycle, . . . trail-bike or mini-bike . . . unless it is equipped with an exhaust system of a type installed as standard equipment, or comparable to that designed for use on that particular vehicle or device as standard factory equipment, in good working order and in constant operation to prevent excessive noise.

Va. Code Ann. § 46.2-1066 (2013). Brakes

Every bicycle, electric power-assisted bicycle, and moped, when operated on a highway, shall be equipped with a brake that will enable the operator to make the braked wheels skid on dry, level, clean pavement.

Va. Code Ann. § 46.2-1078 (2013). Unlawful to operate motor vehicle, bicycle, electric personal assistive mobility device, electric power-assisted bicycle, or moped while using earphones

It shall be unlawful for any person to operate a motor vehicle, bicycle, electric personal assistive mobility device, electric power-assisted bicycle, or moped on the highways in the Commonwealth while using earphones on or in both ears.

For the purpose of this section, "earphones" shall mean any device worn on or in both ears that converts electrical energy to sound waves or which impairs or hinders the person's ability to hear, but shall not include (i) any prosthetic device that aids the hard of hearing, (ii) earphones installed in helmets worn by motorcycle operators and riders and used as part of a communications system, or (iii) nonprosthetic, closed-ear, open-back, electronic noise-cancellation devices designed and used to enhance the hearing ability of persons who operate vehicles in high-noise environments, provided any such device is being worn by the operator of a vehicle with a gross vehicle weight rating of 26,000 pounds or more. The provisions of this section shall not apply to the driver of any emergency vehicle as defined in § 46.2-920.

Va. Code. Ann. § 46.2-1081 (2013). Slow-moving vehicle emblems

E. The provisions of this section shall not apply to bicycles, electric power-assisted bicycles, or mopeds. Display of a slow-moving vehicle emblem on a bicycle, electric power-assisted bicycle, or moped shall not be deemed a violation of this section.

TITLE 46.2. MOTOR VEHICLES (cont'd)
MISC. PROVISIONS

Va. Code Ann. § 46.2-100 (2013). Definitions

The following words and phrases when used in this title shall, for the purpose of this title, have the meanings respectively ascribed to them in this section except in those instances where the context clearly indicates a different meaning:

"Bicycle" means a device propelled solely by human power, upon which a person may ride either on or astride a regular seat attached thereto, having two or more wheels in tandem, including children's bicycles, except a toy vehicle intended for use by young children. For purposes of Chapter 8 (§ 46.2-800 et seq.), a bicycle shall be a vehicle while operated on the highway.

"Bicycle lane" means that portion of a roadway designated by signs and/or pavement markings for the preferential use of bicycles, electric power-assisted bicycles, and mopeds.

"Electric power-assisted bicycle" means a vehicle that travels on not more than three wheels in contact with the ground and is equipped with (i) pedals that allow propulsion by human power and (ii) an electric motor with an input of no more than 1,000 watts that reduces the pedal effort required of the rider. For the purposes of Chapter 8 (§ 46.2-800 et seq.), an electric power-assisted bicycle shall be a vehicle when operated on a highway.

. . . Except as otherwise provided, for the purposes of this title, any device herein defined as a bicycle, electric personal assistive mobility device, electric power-assisted bicycle, or moped shall be deemed not to be a motor vehicle.

"Shared-use path" means a bikeway that is physically separated from motorized vehicular traffic by an open space or barrier and is located either within the highway right-of-way or within a separate right-of-way. Shared-use paths may also be used by pedestrians, skaters, users of wheel chairs or wheel chair conveyances, joggers, and other nonmotorized users.

"Toy vehicle" . . . does not include electric personal assistive mobility devices, electric power-assisted bicycles, mopeds, or motorcycles, nor does it include any nonmotorized or non-propellant-driven devices such as bicycles. . . .

. . . For the purposes of Chapter 8 (§ 46.2-800 et seq.), bicycles, electric personal assistive mobility devices, electric power-assisted bicycles, and mopeds shall be vehicles while operated on a highway.

Va. Code Ann. § 46.2-749.111 (2013). Special license plates for bicycle enthusiasts

On receipt of an application therefor, the Commissioner shall issue special license plates to bicycle enthusiasts.

TITLE 33.1. HIGHWAYS, BRIDGES AND FERRIES
MISC. PROVISIONS

Va. Code Ann. § 33.1-69.001 (2013). Design standards for state secondary highway system components

For urban and urban development areas in jurisdictions using the urban county executive form of government, the Virginia Department of Transportation shall . . . review new design standards for state secondary highway system components. . . . Such standards shall . . . (iv) accommodate safe pedestrian and bicyclist movement. . . .

Va. Code Ann. § 33.1-152.1 (2013). Permissible uses by counties of certain discontinued secondary system highways

. . . The county governing body may by ordinance provide for use of a discontinued highway for any of the following purposes: (i) hiking or bicycle trails and paths or other nonvehicular transportation and recreation purposes. . . .

Va. Code. § 33.1-223 (2013). Fund for access roads and bikeways to public recreational areas and historical sites; construction, maintenance, etc., of such facilities

A. The General Assembly hereby declares it to be in the public interest that access roads and bikeways to public recreational areas and historical sites be provided . . .

C. Upon the setting aside of the funds as herein provided, the Commonwealth Transportation Board shall construct, reconstruct, maintain or improve access roads and bikeways to public recreational areas and historical sites upon the following conditions:

1. When the Director of the Department of Conservation and Recreation has designated a public recreational area as such or when the Director of the Department of Historic Resources has determined a site or area to be historic and recommends to the Commonwealth Transportation Board that an access road or bikeway be provided or maintained to that area;

2. When the Commonwealth Transportation Board pursuant to the recommendation from the Director of the Department of Conservation and Recreation declares by resolution that the access road or bikeway be provided or maintained;

3. When the governing body of the county, city or town in which the access road or bikeway is to be provided or maintained passes a resolution requesting the road; and

4. When the governing body of the county, city or town in which the bikeway is to be provided or maintained adopts an ordinance pursuant to [the appropriate provisions].

No access road or bikeway shall be constructed, reconstructed, maintained or improved on privately owned property.

D. Any access road constructed, reconstructed, maintained or improved pursuant to the provisions of this section shall become part of the primary system of state highways, the secondary system of state highways or the road system of the locality in which it is located in the manner provided by law, and shall thereafter be constructed, reconstructed, maintained and improved as other roads in such systems. Any bikeway path constructed, reconstructed, maintained, or improved pursuant to the provisions of this section which is not situated within the right-of-way limits of an access road which has become, or which is to become, part of the primary system of state highways, the secondary system of state highways, or the road system of the locality, shall, upon completion, become part of and be regulated and maintained by the authority or agency maintaining the public recreational area or historical site. It shall be the responsibility of the authority, agency, or locality requesting that a bicycle path be provided for a public recreational or historical site to provide the right-of-way needed for the construction, reconstruction, maintenance, or improvement of the bicycle path if such is to be situated outside the right-of-way limits of an access road. . . .

Va. Code Ann. § 33.1-223.2:6 (2013). Funding and undertaking of pedestrian and/or bicycle projects apart from highway projects not prohibited

Nothing contained in this chapter and no regulation promulgated by the Commissioner of Highways or the Commonwealth Transportation Board shall be construed to prohibit or limit the ability of the Commonwealth Transportation Board or the Department to fund and undertake pedestrian and/or bicycle projects except in conjunction with highway projects.

MISC. PROVISIONS (OTHER)

Va. Code Ann. § 10.1-204 (2013). Statewide system of trails

D. Each trail shall be limited to foot, horse, or nonmotorized bicycle use, or a combination thereof, as deemed appropriate by the Department. The use of motorized vehicles by the public shall be prohibited along any of the scenic, recreation, or connecting or side trails. . . .

. . . Notwithstanding any provision to the contrary, the Department is authorized to permit, in accordance with applicable state and federal laws, the operation of electric power-assisted bicycles and electric personal assistive mobility devices as defined in § 46.2-100 on any bicycle path or trail designated by the Department for such use.

Va. Code Ann. § 10.1-1152 (2013). State Forester may require permits and fees

A. The State Forester is authorized to require any person who . . . rides bikes . . . on any [State Forest land] to obtain a special use permit. A special use permit to engage in these activities on any such lands shall be issued for a fee established by regulations promulgated by the Department.

Va. Code Ann. § 15.2-1720 (2013). Localities authorized to license bicycles, electric power-assisted bicycles, mopeds, and electric personal assistive mobility devices; disposition of unclaimed bicycles, electric power-assisted bicycles, mopeds, and electric personal assistive mobility devices

Any locality may, by ordinance, (i) provide for the public sale or donation to a charitable organization of any bicycle, electric personal assistive mobility device, electric power-assisted bicycle, or moped that has been in the possession of the police or sheriff's department, unclaimed, for more than thirty days; (ii) require every resident owner of a bicycle, electric power-assisted bicycle, electric personal assistive mobility device, or moped to obtain a license therefor and a license plate, tag, or adhesive license decal of such design and material as the ordinance may prescribe, to be substantially attached to the bicycle, electric personal assistive mobility device, electric power-assisted bicycle, or moped; (iii) prescribe the license fee, the license application forms and the license form; and (iv) prescribe penalties for operating a bicycle, electric personal assistive mobility device, electric power-assisted bicycle, or moped on public roads or streets within the locality without an attached license plate, tag, or adhesive decal. The ordinance shall require the license plates, tags, or adhesive decals to be provided by and at the cost of the locality. Any locality may provide that the license plates, tags, or adhesive decals shall be valid for the life of the bicycles, electric personal assistive mobility devices, electric power-assisted bicycles, and mopeds to which they are attached or for such other period as it may prescribe and may prescribe such fee therefor as it may deem reasonable. When any town license is required as provided for herein, the license shall be in lieu of any license required by any county ordinance. Any bicycle, electric personal assistive mobility device, electric power-assisted bicycle, or moped found and delivered to the police or sheriff's department by a private person that thereafter remains unclaimed for thirty days after the final date of publication as required herein may be given to the finder; however, the location and description of the bicycle, electric personal assistive mobility device, electric power-assisted bicycle, or moped shall be published at least once a week for two successive weeks in a newspaper of general circulation within the locality. In addition, if there is a license, tag, or adhesive license decal affixed to the bicycle, electric personal assistive mobility device, or electric power-assisted bicycle, or moped, the record owner shall be notified directly.

Va. Code Ann. § 15.2-1806 (2013). Parks, recreation facilities, playgrounds, etc.

B. A locality may also establish, conduct and regulate a system of . . . biking . . . trails and may set apart for such use any land or buildings owned or leased by it and may obtain licenses or permits for such use on land not owned or leased by it.

Va. Code Ann. § 29.1-509 (2013). Duty of care and liability for damages of landowners to [bicyclists]

B. A landowner shall owe no duty of care to keep land or premises safe for entry or use by others for . . . bicycle riding. . . . No landowner shall be required to give any warning of hazardous conditions or uses of, structures on, or activities on such land or premises to any person entering on the land or premises for such purposes, except as provided in subsection D. The provisions of this subsection apply without regard to whether the landowner has given permission to a person to use their land for recreational purposes.

C. Any landowner who gives permission, express or implied, to another person to . . . bicycle . . . upon land or premises for the personal use of such person, or for the use of an easement or license as set forth in subsection B does not thereby:

1. Impliedly or expressly represent that the premises are safe for such purposes; or

2. Constitute the person to whom such permission has been granted an invitee or licensee to whom a duty of care is owed; or

3. Assume responsibility for or incur liability for any intentional or negligent acts of such person or any other person, except as provided in subsection D.

D. Nothing contained in this section, except as provided in subsection E, shall limit the liability of a landowner which may otherwise arise or exist by reason of his gross negligence or willful or malicious failure to guard or warn against a dangerous condition, use, structure, or activity. The provisions of this section shall not limit the liability of a landowner which may otherwise arise or exist when the landowner receives a fee for use of the premises or to engage in any activity described in subsections B and C. . . .

Va. Code Ann. § 58.1-3504 (2013). Classification of certain household goods and personal effects for taxation; governing body may exempt

A. Notwithstanding any provision of § 58.1-3503, household goods and personal effects are hereby defined as separate items of taxation and classified as follows:

1. Bicycles.

The classification above set forth shall apply only to such property owned and used by an individual or by a family or household incident to maintaining an abode.

The governing body of any county, city or town may, by ordinance duly adopted, exempt from taxation all of the above classes of household goods and personal effects.

APPENDIX 1(A)
ALEXANDRIA CODE OF ORDINANCES
TITLE 10. MOTOR VEHICLES AND TRAFFIC

I. Chapter 7. Bicycles

§ 10-7-1. Registration and license tags; fees

The owner of every bicycle kept or regularly operated within the city shall register the same with the police chief and shall obtain from him a license tag for such vehicle, which tag shall be attached and sealed on the rear of the bicycle. The registration and tag shall cost $0.25 and shall be effective throughout the life of the bicycle; except, that in the event of any transfer, the new owner shall obtain a transfer of license tag from the police chief at a cost of $0.10.

§ 10-7-2. Owner's report of change of ownership, etc.

Within 10 days after change of ownership or dismantling and removal from operation of any bicycle, the previous owner shall report the information to the police chief.

§ 10-7-3. Reports required of bicycle dealers

Every person engaged in the business of buying or selling new or secondhand bicycles shall report to the police chief every bicycle purchased or sold by such person, as well as the name and address of the person from whom it is purchased or to whom it is sold, a description of the bicycle by name or make, the frame number thereof, and the number of the license tag, if any, found thereon.

§ 10-7-4. Designation of sidewalks as bicycle routes

With the exception of bicycles operated by police officers in the course of their law enforcement duties, no bicycle shall be operated on any sidewalk in city, except such sidewalks or portions thereof which city council shall by resolution designate as bicycle routes.

§ 10-7-5. Definitions

The following words, when used in this chapter shall, for the purposes of this chapter, have the meanings respectively ascribed to them in this section, except in those instances where the context clearly indicates a different meaning:

(1) Bicycle. Every device propelled by human power upon which any person may ride, having two tandem wheels either of which is over 20 inches in diameter, and including any device generally recognized as a bicycle though equipped with two front or two rear wheels.

(2) Roadway: That portion of a street or highway improved, designed or ordinarily used for vehicular travel. In the event a highway includes two or more separate roadways, the term "roadway" shall refer to any roadway separately but not to all roadways collectively.

(3) Sidewalk. That portion of a street between the curb lines, or the lateral lines of a roadway, and the adjacent property lines intended for the use of pedestrians.

§ 10-7-6. Manner of operating

(a) Every person operating a bicycle upon a roadway shall ride as near to the right side of the roadway as practicable, exercising due care when passing a standing vehicle or one proceeding in the same direction.

(b) Whenever any person shall ride a bicycle on a sidewalk designated by the city council as a bicycle route, the person shall yield the right-of-way to any pedestrian and shall give an audible signal before overtaking and passing any pedestrian or bicycle.

(c) Wherever a bicycle route designated as such pursuant to section 10-7-4 of this chapter is provided adjacent to a roadway, bicycle riders shall use such bicycle route and shall not use the roadway.

§ 10-7-7. Brakes, lights, etc., as prerequisite to registration, etc.

The police chief shall have the authority to refuse to register, license or transfer a tag on any bicycle which is not equipped with effective brakes and with lights and reflectors as required in this title.

§ 10-7-8. Passengers

No bicycle operated in the city shall be used to carry more persons at one time than the number of persons for which it is designed and equipped.

§ 10-7-9. Riding abreast

Persons riding bicycles upon roadways or sidewalks designated by the city council as bicycle routes shall not ride two or more abreast.

§ 10-7-10. Parking

No person shall park a bicycle in the city other than against a curb or in a sidewalk rack or against a building in such manner as to cause the least possible obstruction to traffic.

§ 10-7-11. Warning devices

Every bicycle operated in the city shall be equipped with a bell or other device capable of giving a signal audible for a distance of at least 100 feet; except, that no bicycle shall be equipped with any siren or whistle.

§ 10-7-12. Bicycle helmets

(a) Requirement. Every person 14 years of age or younger shall wear a protective helmet when riding or being carried on a bicycle on any roadway, sidewalk or public bicycle path within the city. For the purpose of this section, "protective helmet" shall refer to any helmet that meets the standards promulgated by the American National Standards Institute or the Snell Memorial Foundation.

(b) Civil penalty. The parents of any person who violates this section shall be, jointly and severally, liable for a civil penalty. For each such violation, the parents of the violator shall be liable for a penalty of $25; provided, that such penalty shall be suspended (i) for any person's first violation and (ii) for any person's second or subsequent violation, if the person provides proof of ownership of, or of having purchased or acquired, subsequent to the violation but prior to the deadline for payment of the civil penalty, a helmet of the type required by this section.

(c) Procedures. If a violation of this section has occurred, the violator shall be given written notice of the violation. The notice shall state:

(1) that the parents of the violator shall be liable for the civil penalty set forth in subsection (b);

(2) the circumstances under which the civil penalty may be suspended, as provided in subsection (b); and

(3) the deadline by which the parents of the violator must appear, either in person or by mail, before the treasurer of the city and admit liability for or plead no contest to the violation, and pay the civil penalty

established for the violation, or alternatively provide satisfactory proof of ownership, purchase or acquisition, within the time specified in subsection (b), of a helmet of the type required by subsection (a).

An admission of liability or a statement of no contest to a violation of this section shall not be deemed a criminal violation for any purpose. If the parents of a violator do not elect to admit liability or plead no contest, the violation shall be tried in the Alexandria General District Court upon the filing of a warrant in debt.

II. Chapter 3. Operation of Vehicles

§ 10-3-7. Driving on sidewalks

No person shall drive any vehicle, including bicycles, mopeds and motorcycles, upon any sidewalk except while actually crossing the sidewalk at a temporary or permanent driveway. As used in this section, "sidewalk" means any public sidewalk or pedestrian walkway, park, square or plaza in the city; and any private sidewalk or pedestrian walkway, park, square or plaza in the city to which the general public is regularly afforded access by easement, invitation or license.

§ 10-3-903. Riding or driving vehicles other than bicycles on sidewalks

Pursuant to the authority granted by section 46.2-1313 of the Code of Virginia (1950), as amended, section 46.2-903 of the

Virginia Code, as amended, which relates to riding or driving vehicles other than bicycles on sidewalks, is hereby adopted and incorporated in its entirety into this chapter as if it were fully set forth herein.

§ 10-3-1078. Unlawful to operate a motor vehicle, moped or bicycle while using earphones

Pursuant to the authority granted by section 46.2-1313 of the Code of Virginia (1950), as amended, section 46.2-1078 of the Virginia Code, as amended, which prohibits operating a motor vehicle, moped or bicycle while using earphones, is hereby adopted and incorporated in its entirety into this chapter as if it were fully set forth herein.

III. <u>Miscellaneous</u>

§ 10-1-16. Clinging to moving vehicles

Any person riding upon any bicycle . . . shall not attach the same or himself to any moving vehicle upon any roadway.

§ 10-5-1. Playing on streets and sidewalks—generally

No person shall play on a street, other than upon the sidewalks thereof, within the city, or use in play thereon [certain specified wheeled vehicles] except bicycles, tricycles and motorcycles. . . .

TITLE 5. TRANSPORTATION AND ENVIRONMENTAL SERVICES
CHAPTER 2. STREETS AND SIDEWALKS

§ 5-2-19. Sale of articles of commerce from vehicles prohibited or limited while parking on city streets

It shall be unlawful for any person to offer for sale or sell any goods, wares, merchandise, foodstuffs or similar items from a vehicle or trailer that is parked, placed or stopped on a city street alongside of or next to a parking meter. . . . Notwithstanding this prohibition, a display of bicycles offered for rent from the public right of way pursuant to section 7-2400 of the zoning ordinance and section 5-2-29(g) is permitted.

§ 5-2-29. Rental bicycles.

(g) Bicycles offered for rent may be displayed and rented from areas of right of way pursuant to section 7-2400 of the zoning ordinance and this section 5-2-29.

(h) Encroachment requirements. In addition to any other restrictions or requirements imposed by this code or the City of Alexandria Zoning Ordinance, the owner of any . . . bicycle display or similar street furniture that encroaches into a public right-of-way pursuant to this section shall also comply with the following:

(1) Liability insurance. The owner shall obtain and maintain a policy of general liability insurance in the amount of $1,000,000 which will indemnify the owner (and all succes-

sors in interest), and the city as an additional named insured, against all claims, demands, suits and related costs, including attorneys' fees, arising from any bodily injury or property damage which may occur as a result of the encroachment.

(2) Removal of encroachment. The owner or any successor in interest shall remove the encroachment if the city determines that the encroachment interferes with public access or is otherwise inconsistent with the public welfare. In such case, the city shall provide the owner or successor in interest with written notice of the need to remove the encroachment at least 10 days prior to the date on which the removal must be completed. If the owner or successor in interest cannot be found, or fails to remove the encroachment within the time specified, the city shall have the right to remove the encroachment, at the expense of the owner or successor, and shall not be liable for any loss or damage to the encroaching structure that may occur as a result of the removal.

TITLE 6. PARKS, RECREATION AND CULTURAL ACTIVITIES

§ 6-1-4. Market Square—prohibited conduct: Riding mopeds, skateboards, or bicycles; [etc.]

(a) It shall be unlawful for any person to ride any moped, skateboard, or bicycle . . . at any place within the city's public area known as Market Square, which square lies between the 100 blocks of North Royal and North Fairfax Streets, bounded on the south side by King Street and on the north by city hall;

provided further, that this section shall not be construed to prohibit public employees or their duly authorized agents from using or operating motor vehicles in Market Square in the performance of their duties.

§ 6-1-6. The publicly owned open space east of the eastern right-of-way line of North Union Street, south of the southern right-of-way line of Thompson's Alley, north of the northern right-of-way line of King Street and west of the pierhead line in the Potomac River—prohibited conduct: Riding mopeds, skateboards, on bicycles; [etc.]

(a) It shall be unlawful for any person to ride any moped, skateboard, or bicycle . . . at any place within the city's public open space lying east of the eastern right-of-way line of North Union Street, south of the southern right-of-way line of Thompson's Alley, north of the northern right-of-way line of King Street and west of the pierhead line in the Potomac River; provided further, that this section shall not be construed to prohibit public employees or their duly authorized agents from using or operating motor vehicles in said public space in the performance of their duties.

§ 6-1-8. Conduct prohibited by official sign

(a) Within the boundary of any public park in the city, it shall be unlawful for any person, contrary to an official sign, to:

(11) ride or operate any bicycle, except on designated bike paths; provided, that this provision shall not apply to law en-

forcement personnel. . . .

(b) It shall also be unlawful for any person, after having been specifically directed by a police officer, or by an employee of the department of recreation, parks, and cultural activities who is authorized to enforce this section, to cease engaging in conduct that is unlawful under subsection (a), to refuse or fail to cease engaging in the conduct.

(f) Enforcement and penalties:

(1) This section shall be enforced by any police officer, and, in addition, by any employee of the department of recreation, parks, and cultural activities authorized in writing by the city manager to enforce this section.

(2) Any violation of the provisions of subsection (a) shall be punished as a class four misdemeanor.

(3) Any violation of the provisions of subsection (b) shall be punished as a class two misdemeanor.

MISC. REGULATIONS

§ 3-2-231. Certain tangible personal property exempt from tax

The following classes of household goods and personal effects shall be exempt from the tax on tangible personal property. This exemption shall apply only to property that is owned and used by an individual or a family or household incident to maintaining an abode.

(1) bicycles

§ 4-1-16. Sale, donation, or use of property not returned

(b) Any bicycle or moped which has been in the possession of the police department and unclaimed for more than 60 days may, at the discretion of the chief, be disposed of by donation to a charitable organization. Prior to such donation and subsequent to the 60-day period required by this subsection, the chief shall cause an advertisement to be inserted once a week for two successive weeks in a newspaper having general circulation in the city. The advertisement shall describe the property with reasonable certainty and shall state that, unless the property is claimed by the owner, with satisfactory proof of ownership, before a specified time and date, the property may be donated to a charitable organization.

APPENDIX 1(B)
ARLINGTON COUNTY REGULATIONS
ARLINGTON COUNTY CODE
CHAPTER 14.2. MOTOR VEHICLES AND TRAFFIC

I. Article II. Bicycles

§ 14.2-62. License and registration

A. An owner may voluntarily register his bicycle with the County.

B. Application for registration of ownership and a license will be made to the County upon a form prescribed by the County Manager.

C. Upon receipt of such application in proper form, the County shall provide, at the expense of the

County, a tag bearing the number of the license issued, which should be securely attached at the time of issuance, or upon receipt, to the bicycle.

D. Substitute for lost or mutilated tags shall be issued to a person entitled thereto upon furnishing satisfactory information.

E. It shall be the duty of the County Manager or his designee to keep a record of the issuance of each bicycle license, showing the registration number and license number of each bicycle, the name and address of the licensee, and such other description of the bicycle as the County Manager deems necessary for the administration of this section.

§ 14.2-62.1. Disposition of unclaimed bicycles or mopeds

A. If any bicycle or moped is found and delivered to the Police Department, the Police Department shall, within a reasonable time, attempt to notify the owner and return the bicycle or moped to him. If the bicycle has a County bicycle tag affixed, then the recorded owner shall be notified directly.

B. If any bicycle or moped is found and delivered to the Police Department by a private person and remains unclaimed for thirty (30) days after the location and description of the bicycle or moped has been published at least once a week for two (2) successive weeks in a newspaper of general circulation within the County, the bicycle or moped shall be given to the finder.

C. If any bicycle or moped remains in the possession of the Police Department unclaimed for more than thirty (30) days and the finder has not requested that it be given to him, the Police Department shall dispose of it by public sale or donate it to a charitable organization located in Arlington County which has made written request to the Chief of Police. The Chief of Police or his designee shall have sole discretion to determine disposition of property under this provision.

§ 14.2-63. Defacing or removing serial numbers

A. It shall be unlawful for any person to deface, remove, or modify from any bicycle the serial number imprinted thereon.

B. It shall be unlawful to sell or purchase any bicycle on which the serial number or identification number has been defaced, removed, or modified without first registering same as provided in § 14.2-62.

§ 14.2-64. Equipment requirements

A. Every person fourteen (14) years of age or younger shall wear a protective helmet that meets the standards promulgated by the American National Standards Institute in the American National Standard for Protective Headgear for Bicyclists approved on March 12, 1984, or the Snell Memorial Foundations' 1990 Standard for Protective Headgear, whenever riding or being carried on a bicycle on any highway as defined in [Code of Virginia, §] 46.2-100, sidewalk, or public bicycle path. A copy of these standards are kept on file in the office of the Police Department's Staff Support Section and may be examined from 8:00 a.m. until 4:00 p.m. on regular business days.

B. Violation of subsection A shall be punishable by a fine of twenty-five dollars ($25.00). However, such fine shall be suspended (i) for first-time violators and (ii) for violators who, subsequent to the violation but prior to imposition of the fine, purchase helmets of the type required by this section.

§ 14.2-64.1. Establishment of bicycle paths and regulation of the use thereof

A. The existing and approved bike trails designated on the Arlington Bicycle Transportation Plan, adopted by the County Board of which not fewer than three (3) copies have been and are now filed in the office of the Clerk of the County Board and the Department of Environmental Services and may be viewed there during regular business hours on their regular business days, and the same is hereby adopted and incorporated as fully as if set our at length herein and such trails are hereby established as the bicycle paths of Arlington County.

B. The use of such off-street bicycle paths by persons operating vehicles other than bicycles is prohibited and violations of this section shall be a misdemeanor. "Vehicle" as used herein means any motorized vehicle powered by an internal combustion engine, electrical motor, or other electrical device. The prohibition of this section shall not apply to County or park authority vehicles entering the off-street bicycle paths for maintenance, fire, and police patrol purposes.

C. The prohibitions of this section do not apply to vehicles being used by handicapped persons when such use is necessary because of the handicapped condition of the person or persons using such vehicles.

§ 14.2-65. Riding and parking regulations

Every person riding a bicycle upon a roadway has all the rights and is subject to all the duties applicable to the driver of a motor vehicle except those provisions which by their very nature can have no application.

A. Speed. No bicycle shall be ridden faster than is reasonable and proper, but every bicycle shall be operated with reasonable regard for the safety of the operator and every other person upon the streets and sidewalks of the County.

B. Observation of traffic regulations. Every person riding or propelling a bicycle on any public highway in the County shall observe all authorized traffic signs, signals, and traffic-control devices. Whenever signs are erected indicating that no right or left or U-turn is permitted, no person operating a bicycle shall disobey the direction of any such signs, except where such person dismounts from the bicycle to make any such movements or turns, in which event such person shall then obey the regulation applicable to pedestrians.

C. Stop signs. All persons riding a bicycle on a sidewalk or a public highway shall stop at all stop signs.

D. Riding on bicycles. No person propelling a bicycle shall permit any person to ride on the handlebars.

E. Riding on sidewalk. Persons of any age may ride a bicycle upon any sidewalk, except for those sidewalks, designated by the County Manager on which bicycle riding is prohibited. Signs indicating such prohibition shall be conspicuously posted in general areas where bicycle riding is prohibited.

F. Bicycle lane. Where the County Board has by ordinance designated a bicycle lane for the exclusive use of bicycles, a motor vehicle may cross a bicycle lane for the purpose of entering or exiting adjacent property, for making a turn, or for the purpose of parking, but no person shall stop, stand or park a motor vehicle in a bicycle lane, nor shall any person drive a motor vehicle in a bicycle lane for a distance of more than one hundred (100) feet.

G. Parking. No person shall stand or park a bicycle upon the street other than upon the street roadway against the curb. No person shall stand or park a bicycle upon the sidewalk other than in a rack to support the bicycle, or attached to a streets sign, or light post, or against a building, or at the curb, at back edge of the sidewalk. This will be done in such a manner as to afford the least obstruction to pedestrian and vehicular traffic.

§ 14.2-65.1. Designation of bicycle lanes

The County Board hereby establishes bicycle lanes upon and along the following streets, at the following locations, which lanes shall be of such dimensions as determined by the County Manager and which lanes shall be for the exclusive use of bicyclists:

- Patrick Henry Drive between Wilson Boulevard and North George Mason Drive.
- North Rhodes Street between Arlington Boulevard and Wilson Boulevard.
- North Scott Street between Lee Highway and Key Boulevard.
- Key Boulevard between North Scott Street and North Nash Street.
- Yorktown Boulevard between North George Mason Drive and 26th Street North.
- North Veitch Street between Lee Highway and Wilson Boulevard.
- South Eads Street between South Glebe Road and 23rd Street South.
- South Abingdon Street between 31st Street South and 34th Street South.
- 34th Street South between South Abingdon Street and South Stafford Street.
- South Stafford Street between 32nd Road and 34th Street South.

- Wilson Boulevard between North Oak Street and North Washington Boulevard.
- Clarendon Boulevard between North Washington Boulevard and North Oak Street.
- Fairfax Drive between North Glebe Road and Wilson Boulevard.
- 15th Street South between Crystal Drive and South Joyce Street.
- South Hayes Street between Army Navy Drive and 18th Street South.
- 18th Street South between South Eads Street and South Hayes Street.
- North Pershing Drive between North Washington Boulevard and Arlington Boulevard.
- Walter Reed Drive southbound between South Pollard Street and South Four Mile Run Drive.
- South Randolph Street between South Arlington Mill Drive and 31st Street South.
- North Quincy Street between Lee Highway and Wilson Boulevard.
- Nelly Custis Drive between Lorcom Lane and Military Road.

- Military Road between Nelly Custis Drive and North Old Glebe Road.
- North Ohio Street/McKinley Road between North Washington Boulevard and Wilson Boulevard.
- Yorktown Boulevard between North George Mason Drive and Little Falls Road.
- John Marshall Drive between North Little Falls Road and Lee Highway.
- Lorcom Lane between Military Road and North Edgewood Street.
- Crystal Drive between 27th Street South and 15th Street South.
- Lee Highway between North Quincy Street and North Kenmore Street.
- North George Mason Drive between Wilson Boulevard and 10th Street North.
- Williamsburg Boulevard between North Glebe Road and Westmoreland Street.
- Old Dominion Drive between Lee Highway and 26th Street North.
- Kirkwood Road between Washington Boulevard and Lee Highway.

§ 14.2-66. Penalties

It shall be unlawful to violate any of the prohibitions of § 14.2-63. Any person who violates any of these provisions shall be punished by a fine of not more than two hundred dollars ($200.00).

II. Miscellaneous

§ 14.2-24. Playing on streets or highways; skating, roller coasters, etc.; County Manager may close streets for coasting, etc.

A. No person shall use on a highway or street in said County, [certain specified] devices on wheels or runners . . . except bicycles and motorcycles. . . .

B. No person riding upon any bicycle . . . or other devices [on] wheels or runners shall attach the same or himself to any vehicle upon a roadway.

§ 14.2-25. Penalty for violating § 14.2-24

Any person convicted of violating any of the provisions of § 14.2-24 shall be fined not less than two dollars ($2.00) nor more than twenty-five dollars ($25.00) for each offense.

§ 14.2-80. Prohibited conduct

A. For the purposes of this article, and unless otherwise specified herein, a "rail transit station" is a regular rail stopping place for the pick-up and discharge of passengers in regular route service, contract service, special or community type service, including the fare-paid areas and roofed areas of the rail transit stations (not bus terminals or bus stops) owned, operated, or controlled by the Washington Metropolitan Area Transit Authority (WMATA).

It shall be unlawful for passengers or occupants, while aboard a public passenger vehicle, including buses and rapid rail passenger cars capable of seating twelve (12) or more passengers, owned, operated, or controlled by WMATA while said public passenger vehicle is transporting passengers in regular route service, contract service, special or community type service, or any person in a rail transit station owned, operated, or controlled by WMATA to:

1. Park, operate, carry, wheel or chain to any fence, tree, railing, or other structure not specifically designated for such use, or cause to be parked, operated, carried, wheeled, or chained to any fence, tree, railing or other structure not specifically designed for such use, bicycles, tricycles, unicycles, mopeds, motor bikes, or any other such vehicle, unless said person has in his possession a valid current permit issued by WMATA for the transporting of non-collapsible bicycles by rail transit and said person is complying with all terms and conditions of said permit.

CHAPTER 11. LICENSES

§ 11-59. Business service occupations

Every person engaging in any of the following business services shall pay an annual license tax of thirty-five cents ($0.35) for each one hundred dollars ($100.00) of gross receipts from the business during the preceding calendar year:

. . . Renting bicycles . . .

§ 11-60. Repair service occupations

Every person engaging in any of the following repair services shall pay an annual license tax of thirty-five cents ($0.35) for each one hundred dollars ($100.00) of gross receipts from the business during the preceding calendar year:

. . . Bicycle repair . . .

§ 11-61. Retail merchants

Every person engaging in any of the following retail businesses shall pay an annual license tax of twenty cents ($0.20) for each one hundred dollars ($100.00) of gross receipts from the business during the preceding calendar year:

. . . Bicycles . . .

APPENDIX 1(C)
FAIRFAX COUNTY REGULATIONS
FAIRFAX COUNTY CODE
CHAPTER 82. MOTOR VEHICLES AND TRAFFIC

I. Article 1. In General

§ 82-1-2. Definitions

(a) The following words and phrases, when used in this Chapter, shall, for the purpose of this Chapter, have the meanings respectively ascribed to them in this Section, except in those instances where the context clearly indicates a different meaning:

(2) Bicycle shall include pedal bicycles with helper motors rated less than one brake horsepower, which produce only ordinary pedaling speeds up to a maximum of twenty (20) miles per hour, provided such bicycles so equipped shall not be operated upon any highway or public vehicular area of this State by any person under the age of sixteen (16) years.

(24) Motor vehicle. . . . For the purpose of this Chapter, any device herein defined as a bicycle shall be deemed not to be a motor vehicle.

(53) Vehicle. Every device in, upon or by which any person or property is or may be transported or drawn upon a highway, except devices moved by human power or used exclusively upon stationary rails or tracks and except any vehicle as may be included within the term bicycle as herein defined.

§ 82-1-14. Persons riding bicycles or animals or driving animals subject to provisions of Chapter

Every person riding a bicycle . . . upon a roadway . . . shall be subject to the provisions of this Chapter and shall have all of the rights and all of the duties applicable to the driver of a vehicle, unless the context of the provision clearly indicates otherwise.

§ 82-1-23. Persons operating and riding upon motorcycles or bicycles

A person operating a motorcycle or bicycle shall ride only upon the permanent and regular seat attached to such vehicle, and such operator shall not carry any other person, and no other person shall ride on such vehicle unless it is designed to carry more than one (1) person, in which event a passenger may ride upon the permanent and regular seat if designed for two (2) persons, or upon another seat firmly attached to the rear or side of the seat of the operator.

II. Article 6. Equipment

§ 82-6-1. Breakers

(b) Every bicycle when operated upon a highway shall be equipped with a brake which shall enable the operator to make the braked wheels skid on dry, level, clean pavement.

§ 82-6-38.1. Use of a protective helmet while operating a bicycle

Any person under the age of fifteen years of age shall wear a protective helmet that meets the standards promulgated by the American National Standards Institute or the Snell Memorial Foundation while riding or being carried on a bicycle on any highway, sidewalk, or public bicycle path. The term "highway" has the meaning set forth in Code of Virginia, Section 46.2-100. Any person who violates this section shall be punishable by a fine of twenty-five dollars. However, such a fine shall be suspended for first-time violators and for violators who, subsequent to the violation but prior to imposition of the fine, purchase helmets of the type required by this section.

A violation of this section shall not constitute negligence, assumption of risk, be considered in mitigation of damages of whatever nature, be admissible in evidence, or be the subject of comment by counsel in any action for the recovery of damages arising out of operation of any bicycle, nor shall anything in this section change any existing law, rule, or procedure pertaining to any civil action.

§ 82-6-43. Lamps on bicycles

Every bicycle, when in use between sunset and sunrise, shall be equipped with a lamp on the front which shall emit a white light visible in clear weather from a distance of at least five hundred (500) feet to the front and with a red reflector on the rear of a type approved by the Superintendent which shall be visible from all distances in clear weather from fifty (50) feet to three hundred (300) feet to the rear when directly in front of lawful upper beams of head lamps on a motor vehicle. A lamp emitting a red light visible in clear weather from a distance of five hundred (500) feet to the rear may be used in lieu of or in addition to the red reflector.

III. Miscellaneous

§ 82-5-39. Regulation of parking in areas owned/operated by Washington Metropolitan Area Transit Authority (WMATA); authority; penalties for violation

(a) It shall be unlawful, while in or on a parking lot, garage or other facility owned, operated or controlled by WMATA and designated by WMATA for the parking of motor vehicles, mopeds or bicycles by either patrons or employees within Fairfax County to:

(9) Cause to be operated bicycles, skateboards, minibikes, mopeds, trail bikes or any other wheeled vehicle in or on the parking lot, garage or other facility, except when the wheeled vehicle is being parked in accordance with public parking ordinances.

(10) Fail or refuse to leave any parking lot, garage or other facility after being ordered to do so by the attendant or other designated agent of WMATA or a Fairfax County police officer.

(b) Any person violating the provisions of this Section shall be punished by a fine established in accordance with Section

82-1-32.[25]

(c) Unless otherwise provided herein, all provisions of the statutes of the Commonwealth of Virginia, County of Fairfax, relating to public parking, including but not limited to public streets, public alleyways, fire lanes, fire zones, public sidewalks, public parking facilities, and/or public buildings are applicable to the parking facilities, parking lots, parking garages and other facilities designed by WMATA as parking facilities for the parking of all motor vehicles, mopeds or bicycles, and owned, operated or controlled by WMATA.

§ 82-9-6. Playing on streets or highways; roller skates, toys or devices on wheels or runners; use of motor powered vehicles on sidewalks and other posted property; persons riding bicycles, etc.

[25] § 82-1-32. Supplemental enforcement of parking
For [uncontested citations pursuant to § 82-5-39] the fee fine shall be $50.00.
Within 21 days from the day of the issuance of any notice of parking violation described herein, any owner of the vehicle upon which a violation has been issued shall either (1) tender payment of the fee listed above . . . or (2) advise the Director of Tax Administration or the designee of the Director that the person who was issued the violation wishes to contest that violation in the appropriate court of law. Except for instances when the failure to pay or so notify the Director is determined by the Director not to be the fault of the person issued the notice of violation, the Director shall impose a late fee of $25.00 to the owner(s) of any vehicle who neither tenders payment nor notifies the Director that the person wishes to contest the violation within the 21-day period described herein. Furthermore, except as otherwise directed by an appropriate court order, any person who fails to notify the Director or the designee of the Director within 21 days from the date the violation was issued that he or she wishes to contest that violation in court, shall have waived the right to any such contest.

(b) It shall be unlawful for any person to use on a street or highway roller skates, toys or other devices on wheels or runners, except that any bicycle, electric personal assistive mobility device, electric power-assisted bicycle, or moped may be operated on a street or highway in accordance with Virginia Code Section 46.2-905.

(c) It shall further be unlawful for any person to ride (1) a bicycle or other similar such wheeled, rider-propelled device [or] (3) an electric power-assisted bicycle on sidewalks where such activity has been prohibited. Signs indicating such prohibition shall be conspicuously posted in general areas where the riding of such devices is prohibited; provided, that this Section shall not be deemed to prohibit the ordinary use of devices for the assistance of the physically handicapped or bicycles and similar rider-propelled devices used by police officers in furtherance of their duties.

(d) For purposes of this Section, the term "sidewalk" shall be deemed to include any privately owned system of defined pedestrian ways, when the owner thereof shall have requested in writing that the governing body treat such private pedestrian ways as sidewalks for purposes of this Section, and such owner posts notice of that fact at typical points of access from the public right-of-way to such privately owned systems of pedestrian ways. Such owner may request such treatment with respect to some or all of the devices prohibited by this Section, and notices required hereby shall describe the devices prohibited on such privately owned system of walkways.

MISC. RULES

§ 2-2-2. Sale or donation of unclaimed bicycles

Any bicycle not necessary to any court action seized or taken into possession by the Police or Sheriff's Department which has been in the possession of the Police or Sheriff's Department, unclaimed, for more than seventy (70) days (as set forth in Fairfax County Code § 2-2-1(a), (b)) may be sold at public auction or donated to a charitable organization, provided more than three (3) days have passed since the purchasing agent has caused to be published at least once a week for two (2) successive weeks in newspapers of general circulation within the County, the location and description of the bicycle. Where a bicycle seized or taken into possession by the Police or Sheriff's Department is necessary to court action, the above time periods shall begin to run as of the date of final disposition of said action.

§ 85-1-3. Conduct on public vehicle regulated; penalty

(a) It shall be unlawful for passengers or occupants, while aboard a public passenger vehicle not used primarily for the transportation of schoolchildren while said public passenger vehicle is transporting passengers in regular route service, contract service, special or community-type service, or any person in a rail transit station to:

(10) Park, operate, carry or wheel or chain to any fence, railing or other structure, or cause to be parked, operated carried or

wheeled or chained to any fence, railing or other structure, bicycles, tricycles, unicycles, mopeds, motorbikes or any motor-driven vehicle. . . .

(b) Violation of any provisions of this Section shall be punishable by a fine of not less than Five Dollars ($5.00) nor more than Twenty-five Dollars ($25.00) for each offense.

APPENDIX 1(D)
CITY OF FAIRFAX
CODE OF ORDINANCES
CHAPTER 98. TRAFFIC AND VEHICLES

§ 98-9. Riding bicycles without using handlebars

No person shall ride a bicycle upon any street without having his hands upon the handlebars.

§ 98-15. Vehicles on sidewalks

It shall be unlawful for any person to ride or drive any vehicle, including bicycles and motorcycles, on the sidewalks of the city; provided that the city reserves the right to authorize the riding of bicycles upon the sidewalks in certain areas the city may designate as bicycle routes.

§ 98-17. Playing on highways; roller skates, skate boards, toys, or other devices on wheels or runners; persons riding bicycles, electric personal assistive mobility devices, electric power-assisted bicycles, mopeds etc., not to attach to vehicles; exception

(a) No person shall play on a highway, other than on the sidewalks thereof, within the city. No person shall use roller skates, skateboards, toys, or other devices on wheels or runners, except bicycles, electric personal assistive devices, electric power-assisted bicycles, motorized skateboards or scooters, mopeds, and motorcycles, on highways where play is prohibited.

(b) No person riding on any bicycle, electric personal assistive mobility device, electric power-assisted bicycle, moped, roller skates, skateboards, motorized skateboards or scooters, toys, or other devices on wheels or runners, shall attach the same or himself to any vehicle on a roadway.

MISC. REGULATIONS

§ 50-36. Disposition of unclaimed bicycles and mopeds.

(a) Any bicycle or moped which has been in the possession of the police department, unclaimed, for more than 30 days may be disposed of by public sale or donated to a charitable organization; provided, however, that prior to any public sale or donation to a charitable organization, the location and description of the bicycle or moped shall be published at least once a week for two successive weeks in a newspaper of general circulation within the city. In addition, if there is a license tag affixed to the bicycle or moped, the record owner shall be notified directly that the police department has possession of the bicycle or moped and intends to dispose of it by public sale or charitable donation.

(b) Any bicycle or moped found and delivered to the police department by a private person which thereafter remains unclaimed for 30 days after the final date of publication as required herein may be given to the finder.

APPENDIX 1(D)
FALLS CHURCH CODE OF ORDINANCES
CHAPTER 26. MOTOR VEHICLES AND TRAFFIC
ARTICLE IV. BICYCLES

§ 26-105. Definitions

The following words, terms and phrases, when used in this article, shall have the meanings ascribed to them in this section, except where the context clearly indicates a different meaning:

Bicycle means a device upon which any person may ride, propelled by human power through a belt, chain or gears, and having two or three wheels in a tandem or tricycle arrangement. The term "bicycle" shall also include pedal bicycles with helper motors rated less than one brake horsepower, which produce only ordinary pedaling speeds up to a maximum of 20 miles per hour; provided, that such bicycles so equipped shall not be operated upon any highway or public vehicular area of the city by any person under the age of 16 years; provided, further, that no such bicycles so equipped shall be operated upon any public sidewalk or bike trail in the city.

§ 26-106. Defacing or removing serial numbers

(a) It shall be unlawful for any person to deface, modify or remove from any bicycle the serial number imprinted thereon.

(b) It shall be unlawful to sell or purchase any bicycle on which the serial number or identification number has been defaced or removed without first registering same.

§ 26-107. Equipment requirements

(a) No person shall operate a bicycle on streets, sidewalks and bikeways unless it is equipped with coaster brakes or handbrakes in good working condition.

(b) Every bicycle operated upon any street, highway, sidewalk or bikeway during darkness or other periods of restricted visibility shall be equipped, or the operator of such a bicycle shall be equipped, with a front lamp emitting a white light visible from a distance of 500 feet in front of the bicycle and with a red reflector of a type approved by the superintendent of the department of state police, which shall be visible in clear weather from 50 feet to 300 feet to the rear when directly in front of lawful upper beams of head lamps on a motor vehicle. A lamp emitting a red light visible in clear weather from a distance of 500 feet to the rear may be used in addition to the red reflector.

§ 26-108. Bicycle paths

(a) Established. The existing and approved bikeways within the city, which have been established by the Northern Virginia Regional Park Authority or by the city, and any bikeways, which are in the future established by the Northern Virginia Regional Park Authority or the city, are hereby established as the bikeways of the city.

(b) Vehicles prohibited; city and park authority vehicles exempted. The use of off-street bikeways as specified in subsection (a) of this section and/or any sidewalk by any person operating vehicles other than bicycles is unlawful. The term "vehicle," as used herein, means any motorized vehicle powered by an internal combustion engine, electrical motor or other electrical device. The prohibition of this section shall not apply to city or park authority vehicles entering the off-street bikeways for maintenance, fire and police patrol purposes.

(c) Exceptions for vehicles used by handicapped persons. The prohibitions of this section do not apply to vehicles being used by persons with disabilities when such use is necessary because of the handicapped condition of the person using such vehicle.

§ 26-109. Riding and parking regulations

Every person riding a bicycle upon a bikeway, sidewalk, street, highway or roadway has all the rights and is subject to all the duties applicable to the driver of a motor vehicle, except those provisions which by their very nature can have no application. Additionally, every such person shall comply with the following:

(1) Speed. No bicycle shall be operated faster than is reasonable and proper, but every bicycle shall be operated with reasonable regard for the safety of the operator and every other person upon the streets, sidewalks, highways, roadways, and bikeways of the city.

(2) Observation of traffic regulations. Every person riding a bicycle in the city shall observe all authorized traffic signs, signals and traffic control devices. Whenever signs are erected indicating that no right turn or left turn or U-turn is permitted, no person operating a bicycle shall disobey the direction of any such signs, except where such persons dismount from the bicycle to make any such movements or turns; in which event such a person shall then obey the regulation applicable to pedestrians.

(3) Stop signs. All persons operating a bicycle shall stop at all stop signs.

(4) Riding with the traffic flow. Every person operating a bicycle upon a roadway shall ride as near to the right side of the roadway as practical, exercising due care when passing a standing vehicle or one proceeding in the same direction.

(5) Riding on handlebars. No person operating a bicycle shall permit any person to ride on the handlebars.

(6) Interference with control. No person operating a bicycle shall carry any package, bundle, or article which prevents that person from keeping at least one hand firmly upon the handlebars and in full control of the bicycle.

(7) Hitching rides. No person riding upon any bicycle shall attach the same or self to any vehicle on the roadway.

(8) Riding abreast. Bicycles shall be ridden or operated in a single file, except when overtaking a slower moving bicycle, and except on bikeways set aside for the use of bicycles.

(9) Riding on sidewalk. Persons of any age may ride a bicycle upon any sidewalk, except as otherwise prohibited in section 26-110, and except in those areas designated as unsafe by the city manager because of the narrowness of the sidewalk, slope of the sidewalk, number of pedestrians customarily using the sidewalk or potential vehicle conflict.

(10) Pedestrian right-of-way. Whenever any person shall ride a bicycle on the sidewalk or bikeway, whether paved or unpaved, such person shall yield the right-of-way to any pedestrian and shall give an audible signal before overtaking and passing any pedestrian.

(11) Bicycle lane. Where the city council has by ordinance designated a lane for the exclusive use of bicycles, a motor vehicle may enter or cross this lane for the purpose of access to adjacent property or for the purpose of parking, but a motor vehicle shall not be driven in this lane.

(12) Parking. No person shall stand or park a bicycle upon the street, highway, or roadway other than upon the street, highway, or roadway against the curb. No person shall stand or park a bicycle upon the sidewalk or bikeway other than in

a rack to support the bicycle, or against the building, or at the curb, or at the back edge of the sidewalk. This will be done in such a manner as to afford the least obstruction to pedestrian traffic.

(13) Riding on paths adjacent to a roadway. Whenever a usable path or designated bikeway has been provided adjacent to a roadway, bicycle riders shall use such path or bikeway and shall not use the roadway.

(14) Helmet required. Every person 14 years of age or younger shall wear a protective helmet that meets the U.S. Consumer Product Safety Commission safety standard for bicycle helmets, whenever riding or being carried on a bicycle, an electric personal assistive mobility device, a toy vehicle, or an electric power-assisted bicycle on any highway, sidewalk, or public bicycle path.

§ 26-110. Riding or driving on sidewalks

The city manager, upon the request of any owner of any property adjacent to any public sidewalk, may prohibit or restrict the use of such sidewalks by persons riding bicycles; provided such restrictions are posted; and further provided, that children who have not attained their 13th birthday are not prohibited in the first instance from riding bicycles and similar leg-propelled children's devices upon sidewalks. This exception is subject, however, to the right of residents to file complaints of disturbance and to request that the exception herein be modified or set aside in proper cases as found by the court to constitute abuse by such children of pedestrian or neighborhood rights to peace and the use of sidewalks.

§ 26-111. Violations

It shall be unlawful for any person to violate any of the provisions of this article. Any such violation shall, upon conviction, be punishable by a fine of $25.00. In the case of subsection 26-109(14), such fine shall be suspended for first-time violators; and for violators who, subsequent to the violation but prior to imposition of the fine, purchase helmets of the type required by this article. Violators of this article can waive trial and prepay the fine.

MISC. REGULATIONS

§ 28-156. Games in streets

The city council may designate areas on highways under their control where play is permitted and may impose reasonable restrictions on play on such highways. Persons using such devices, except bicycles, electric personal assistive mobility devices, electric power-assisted bicycles, mopeds, and motorcycles, shall keep as near as safely practicable to the far right side or edge of the right traffic lane so they will be proceeding in the same direction as other traffic. No person riding on any bicycle, electric personal assistive mobility device, electric power-assisted bicycle, moped . . . or other devices on wheels or runners shall attach the same or self to any vehicle on a highway.

§ 40-31. Personal property exempt from taxes

(a) There is hereby exempt from taxation the following classes of household goods and personal effects:

(1) Bicycles. . . .

(b) The classification set forth in subsection (a) of this section shall apply only to such property owned and used by an individual or by a family or household incident to maintaining an abode.

APPENDIX 1(E)
PRINCE WILLIAM COUNTY CODE OF ORDINANCES
CHAPTER 13. MOTOR VEHICLES AND TRAFFIC

I. Article XIII. Riding on Bicycles
§ 13-375. Application of traffic regulations to riders

(a) Every person riding a bicycle, electric power-assisted bicycle or moped upon a roadway shall be subject to the provisions of this chapter applicable to the driver of a vehicle, except those provisions which, by their very nature, can have no application.

(b) The provisions of subsections (a) and (c) [of] Code of Virginia, § 46.2-920, and section 13-6[26] of this chapter, applicable to operation of emergency vehicles under emergency conditions shall also apply, mutatis mutandis, to bicycles, electric power-assisted bicycles and mopeds operated under similar emergency conditions of law enforcement officers.

---

[26] § 13-6. Exemptions for operators of emergency vehicles

(a) The driver of any emergency vehicle, when such vehicle is being used in the performance of public services and when such vehicle is operated under emergency conditions, may, without subjecting himself to criminal prosecution:

(1) Disregard speed limits, while having due regard for safety of persons and property;

(2) Proceed past any steady or flashing red signal, traffic light, stop sign or device indicating moving traffic shall stop if the speed of the vehicle is sufficiently reduced to enable it to pass a signal, traffic light, or device with due regard to the safety of persons and property;

(3) Park or stop notwithstanding the other provisions of this chapter;

(4) Disregard regulations governing a direction of movement of vehicles turning in specified directions, so long as the operator does not endanger life or property;

(5) Pass or overtake, with due regard to the safety of persons and property, another vehicle at any intersection;

(6) Pass or overtake, with due regard to the safety of persons and property, while en route to an emergency, stopped or slow-moving vehicles, by going to the left of the stopped or slow-moving vehicle either in a no-passing zone or by crossing the highway centerline; and

(7) Pass or overtake, with due regard to the safety of persons and property, while en route to an emergency, stopped or slow-moving vehicles, by going off the paved or main traveled portion of the roadway on the right. Notwithstanding other provisions of this section, vehicles exempted in this instance will not be required to sound a siren or any device to give automatically intermittent signals.

(c) The exemptions granted by this section shall not protect the operator of any such vehicle from criminal prosecution for conduct constituting reckless disregard of the safety of persons and property. Nothing in this section shall release the operator of any such vehicle from civil liability for failure to use reasonable care in such operation.

(c) Any person operating a bicycle, electric power-assisted bicycle or moped upon a roadway shall be subject to the provisions of this chapter applicable to the driver of a vehicle, except those provisions which, by their very nature, can have no application.

(d) Any person operating a bicycle, electric power-assisted bicycle, or moped upon a roadway at less than the normal speed of traffic at the time and place under conditions then existing shall ride as close as safely practicable to the right-hand curb or edge of the roadway, except under any of the following circumstances:

(1) When overtaking and passing another vehicle proceeding in the same direction;

(2) When preparing for a left turn at an intersection or into private road or driveway;

(3) When reasonably necessary to avoid conditions, including, but not limited to, fixed or moving objects, parked or moving vehicles, pedestrians, animals, surface hazards, or substandard width lanes that make it unsafe to continue along the right-hand curb or edge;

(4) When avoiding riding in a lane that must turn or diverge to the right; and

(5) When riding upon a one-way road or highway, a person may also ride as near the left-hand curb or edge of such roadway as safely practicable.

For purposes of this section, a "substandard width lane" is a lane too narrow for a bicycle, electric power-assisted bicycle, motorized skateboard or scooter, or moped and another vehicle to pass safely side by side within the lane.

Persons riding bicycles, electric personal assistive mobility devices, or electric power-assisted bicycles on a highway shall not ride more than two abreast. Persons riding two abreast shall not impede the normal and reasonable movement of traffic, shall move into a single file formation as quickly as is practicable when being overtaken from the rear by a faster moving vehicle, and, on a laned roadway, shall ride in a single lane.

§ 13-376. Rider to have at least one hand on handlebars

No person operating a bicycle, electric personal assistive mobility device, electric power-assisted bicycle, or moped on any highway in the county shall carry any package, bundle, or article that prevents the driver from keeping at least one hand on the handlebars.

No bicycle or moped shall be used to carry more persons at one time than the number of persons for which it is designed or is equipped, except that an adult bicycle rider may carry a child less than six years old if such child is securely attached to the bicycle in a seat or trailer designed for carrying children.

§ 13-377. Riding on sidewalks

Bicycles or electric power-assisted bicycles may be ridden on sidewalks in the county as provided in section 13-231 of this chapter.

§ 13-378. Rider not to cling to other vehicle

No person riding on a bicycle, electric personal assistive mobility device, electric power-assisted bicycle, moped, roller skates, skateboards or other devices on wheels or runners, shall attach the same or himself to any vehicle upon a highway.

§ 13-379. Riders required to wear helmets

(a) Every person 14 years of age or younger shall wear a protective helmet that at least meets the consumer product safety commission standard whenever riding or being carried on a bicycle, toy vehicle, or electric power-assisted bicycle on any highway, sidewalk, or public bicycle path. Any parent, guardian, or other legal custodian who knowingly permits his or her child 14 years of age or younger to ride or be carried on a bicycle or electric power-assisted bicycle on any highway, sidewalk or public bicycle path without wearing a protective helmet as required by this section shall be guilty of a violation of this section.

(b) Violation of this section shall be punishable by a fine of $25.00. However, such fine shall be suspended for:

(1) First time violators; and

(2) Violators who, subsequent to the violation but prior to imposition of the fine, purchase helmets of the type required by this section.

(c) Violation of this section shall not constitute negligence, assumption of risk, be considered in mitigation of damages of whatever nature, be admissible in evidence, or be the subject of comment by counsel in any action for the recovery of damages arising out of the operation of any bicycle, electric personal assistive mobility device, toy vehicle, or electric power-assisted bicycle, nor shall anything in this section change any existing law, rule, or procedure pertaining to any civil action.

II. Article IV. Vehicle Equipment

§ 13-127. Lights on bicycles, electric power-assisted bicycles and mopeds

(a) Every bicycle, electric power-assisted bicycle and moped, when in use between sunset and sunrise, shall be equipped with a headlight on the front emitting a white light visible in clear weather from a distance of at least 500 feet to the front and a red reflector visible from a distance of at least 600 feet to the rear when directly in front of lawful lower beams of headlights on a motor vehicle. Such lights and reflectors shall be of types approved by the superintendent.

In addition to the foregoing provisions of this section, a bicycle or its rider may be equipped with lights or reflectors. These lights may be steady burning or blinking.

(b) Every bicycle, or its rider shall be equipped with a taillight on the rear emitting a red light plainly visible in clear weather from a distance of at least 500 feet to the rear when in use between sunset and sunrise and operating on any highway with a speed limit of 35 miles per hour or greater. Any such taillight shall be of a type approved by the superintendent of state police.

§ 13-131.3. Flashing amber, purple, or green warning lights

(a) The following vehicles may be equipped with flashing, blinking, or alternating amber warning lights of types approved by the superintendent of state police:

(17) Vehicles used to lead or provide escorts for bicycle races authorized by the Virginia Department of Transportation or the locality in which the race is being conducted. . . .

(b) Except as otherwise provided in this section, such amber lights shall be lit only when performing the functions which qualify them to be equipped with such lights.

§ 13-151. General requirements [Brakes]

(b) Every bicycle, electric power-assisted bicycle and moped, when operated upon a highway, shall be equipped with a brake which will enable the operator to make the braked wheels skid on a dry, level, clean pavement.

III. Article VI. Operation of Vehicles Generally

§ 13-207.1. Unlawful to operate motor vehicle, moped, bicycle or electric power-assisted bicycle while using earphones

It shall be unlawful for any person to operate a motor vehicle, moped, bicycle or electric power-assisted bicycle on the highways in the county while using earphones on or in both ears.

For the purposes of this section, "earphones" shall mean any device worn on or in both ears which converts electrical energy to sound waves or which impairs or hinders the person's ability to hear, but shall not include (i) any prosthetic device which aids the hard of hearing, (ii) earphones installed in helmets worn by motorcycle operators and riders and used as part of a communications system, or (iii) nonprosthetic, closed-ear, open-back, electronic noise-cancellation devices designed and used to enhance the hearing ability of persons who operate vehicles in high-noise environments, provided any such device is being worn by the operator of a vehicle with a gross weight rating of 26,000 pounds or more. The provisions of this section shall not apply to the driver of any emergency vehicles as defined in section 13-6.

§ 13-212. Passing vehicle proceeding in same direction--Generally

(d) Except as otherwise provided in this section, a person riding a bicycle, electric power-assisted bicycle, motorized skateboard or scooter, or moped shall comply with all rules applicable to the driver of a vehicle when overtaking and passing.[27]

(1) A person riding a bicycle, electric power-assisted bicycle, motorized skateboard or scooter, or moped may overtake and pass another vehicle on either the left or right side, staying in the same lane as the overtaken vehicle, or changing to a different lane, or riding off the roadway as necessary to pass with safety.

(2) A person riding a bicycle, electric power-assisted bicycle, motorized skateboard or scooter, or moped may overtake and pass another vehicle only under conditions which permit the movement to be made with safety.

(3) A person riding a bicycle, electric power-assisted bicycle, motorized skateboard or scooter, or moped shall not travel between two lanes of traffic moving in the same direction, except where one lane is a separate turn lane or a mandatory turn lane.

---

[27] Specifically:

(a) The driver of any vehicle overtaking another vehicle proceeding in the same direction shall pass at least two feet to the left of the overtaken vehicle and shall not again drive to the right side of the highway until safely clear of such overtaken vehicle, except as provided in this article.

(b) The driver of a vehicle shall not drive to the left side of the center line of a highway in overtaking and passing another vehicle proceeding in the same direction, unless such left side is clearly visible and is free of oncoming traffic for a sufficient distance ahead to permit such overtaking and passing to be made in safety.

(e) In approaching or passing a person riding a bicycle, electric power-assisted bicycle, moped, animal or animal-drawn vehicle, the driver of the motor vehicle shall pass at a safe distance and at a reasonable speed.

§ 13-216.1. Left turns by bicycles and mopeds

(a) A person riding a bicycle, electric power-assisted bicycle or moped and intending to turn left shall either follow a course described in section 13-216[28] or in subsection

(b) of this section.

(b) A person riding a bicycle, electric power-assisted bicycle or moped and intending to turn left shall approach the turn as closes a practicable to the right curb or edge of the roadway.

---

[28] § 13-216. Turning movements generally
Except where turning is prohibited, a driver intending to turn at an intersection or other location on any highway shall execute the turn as provided in this section.
(2) Left turns on two-way roadways. At any intersection where traffic is permitted to move in both directions on each roadway entering the intersection, an approach for a left turn shall be made from the right half of the roadway and as close as possible to the roadway's center line, passing to the right of the center line where it enters the intersection. After entering the intersection, the left turn shall be made so as to leave the intersection to the right of the center line of the roadway being entered. Wherever practicable, the left turn shall be made to the left of the center of the intersection.
(3) Left turns on other than two-way roadways. At any intersection where traffic is restricted to one direction on one or more of the roadways, and at any crossover from one roadway of a divided highway to another roadway thereof on which traffic moves in the opposite direction, the driver intending to turn left at any such intersection or crossover shall approach the intersection or crossover in the extreme left lane lawfully available to traffic moving in the direction of travel of such vehicle and, after entering the intersection or crossover, the left turn shall be made so as to leave the intersection or crossover as nearly as practicable in the left lane lawfully available to traffic moving in such direction upon the roadway being entered.

After proceeding across the intersecting roadway, the rider shall comply with traffic signs or signals and continue his turn as close as practicable to the right curb or edge of the roadway being entered.

(c) Notwithstanding the foregoing provisions of this section, the Commonwealth transportation board and local authorities may cause official traffic-control devices to be placed at intersections to direct that a specific course be traveled by turning bicycles, electric power-assisted bicycles and mopeds. When such devices are so placed, no person shall turn a bicycle or moped other than as directed by such devices.

§ 13-231. Driving on sidewalks

No person shall ride or drive any vehicle other than . . . a bicycle . . . [or] electric power-assisted bicycle [among other specified vehicles] on the sidewalks in the county.

IV. Miscellaneous

§ 13-287. Specific instances of reckless driving--Generally

A person shall be guilty of reckless driving who shall:

(c) Pass or attempt to pass two other vehicles abreast, moving in the same direction, except on highways having separate roadways of three or more lanes for each direction of travel, or on designated one-way streets or highways; however, this subsection shall not apply to a motor vehicle passing two other vehicles, in accordance with the provisions of this chapter, when one or both of such other vehicles is a bicycle, electric power-assisted bicycle or moped; nor shall this subsection apply to a bicycle, electric power-assisted bicycle or moped passing two other vehicles in accordance with the provisions of this chapter.

(d) Drive any motor vehicle so as to be abreast of another vehicle in a lane designed for one vehicle, or drive any motor vehicle so as to travel abreast of any other vehicle traveling in a lane designed for one vehicle. . . . [T]his subsection shall not apply to a motor vehicle traveling in the same lane of traffic as a bicycle, electric power-assisted bicycle or moped.

CHAPTER 17. PARKS AND RECREATION

§ 17-23. Bicycles to be ridden only in designated areas

No person shall ride a bicycle in a park, except in areas designated for such use.

§ 17-25. Parking of vehicles

(a) No person shall park a vehicle, including a bicycle, at any place on park property, other than in the regular designated facilities provided for parking, unless directed otherwise by police officers or park attendants. Signs, as posted, shall be observed.

(b) No vehicle shall be parked on any roadway, parking area or other part of a park after the park closing hours, except in areas designated for such purposes, such as camping sites and other such areas.

APPENDIX 2
THE DISTRICT OF COLUMBIA STATUTES
TITLE 50. MOTOR AND NON-MOTOR VEHICLES AND TRAFFIC
SUBTITLE V. NON-MOTORIZED VEHICLES
CHAPTER 16. REGULATION OF BICYCLES

I. General Provisions

D.C. Code § 50-1601 (2013). Findings

The Council of the District of Columbia finds that:

(1) Increased use of bicycles for transportation and recreation will result in improved air quality, reduced levels of noise and traffic congestion, greater energy conservation, lower transportation costs, fewer parking problems, and increased physical fitness.

(2) Bicycle fatalities and accidents can be reduced through broad-based education and facilities improvements.

(3) The promotion of bicycle transportation and safety in the District of Columbia ("District") requires the implementation of a comprehensive bicycle transportation and safety program.

(4) A bicycle office is required to coordinate the comprehensive program.

(5) Disability and death from injuries sustained in bicycling accidents are a serious threat to the health, welfare and safety of District children.

(6) Each year approximately 290 children are involved in fatal

accidents, and nearly 400,000 are injured with varying degrees of severity in bicycle related injuries or crashes.

(7) Head injuries account for over 60% of bicycle related fatalities and 1/3 of bicycle related emergency room visits.

(8) Use of a bicycle helmet is the single, most effective preventive measure of reducing head injuries 85%, and brain injuries or serious disabilities by 88% from bicycle accidents.

(9) Only 15% of bicyclists use proper head protective equipment, and some studies show that bicycle helmet usage for children under 16 years of age ranges from 5% to 15%.

D.C. Code § 50-1602 (2013). Comprehensive Bicycle Transportation and Safety Program

(a) There shall be established in the District of Columbia a Comprehensive Bicycle Transportation and Safety Program to promote the safe and convenient use of the bicycle as a means of transportation and recreation.

(b) The scope of the program shall include, but not be limited to:

(1) Planning and supporting road improvements for bicyclists, such as wide curb lanes, smooth shoulders, bicyclist-oriented signs and signals, and removal of hazards;

(2) Improving access for bicyclists on the road network and on all modes of public transportation;

(3) Monitoring construction and repair projects to ensure that no additional hazards or obstacles to bicyclists are created as the transportation system is built or rebuilt;

(4) Assisting, organizing, and coordinating the planning, design, construction, improvement, repair, and maintenance of bicycle facilities, such as bicycle paths and bicycle lanes, both within and separate from the highway rights-of-way;

(5) Promoting the installation of secure and convenient bicycle parking facilities;

(6) Organizing safety education and training programs for young and adult bicyclists, as well as for motorists, to reduce bicycling accidents and foster safe use of bicycles; and

(7) Promoting effective traffic law enforcement to protect the rights of all road users and to encourage good bicycling habits.

D.C. Code § 50-1603 (2013). Office of Bicycle Transportation and Safety

There shall be established within the Office of the Director of the District Department of Transportation an Office of Bicycle Transportation and Safety to promote the safe and convenient use of the bicycle as a means of transportation and recreation.

(1) The Office shall be headed by a bicycle coordinator who shall be a person with broad knowledge in all aspects of bicycle transportation and safety.

(2) The Office shall be staffed with a minimum of 2 full-time assistant bicycle coordinators who shall have appropriate experience and knowledge of bicycle matters.

(3) The duties of the bicycle coordinator shall include, but not be limited to:

(A) Administering the Comprehensive Bicycle Transportation and Safety Program;

(B) Serving as a contact for federal agencies, the press, civic organizations, and individuals on all matters related to bicycling;

(C) Establishing priorities and programming of bicycle facilities;

(D) Coordinating the District of Columbia's bicycle program with all agencies on matters relating to bicycles, including transportation, recreation, touring, sports and racing, physical fitness, and economic development;

(E) Assisting the Mayor of the District of Columbia ("Mayor"), the Director of the District Department of Transportation, or a District agency in preparing budgetary, legislative, or regulatory proposals which may affect bicycling; and

(F) Evaluating and reporting annually to the Mayor and Director of the Department of Public Works on the District's bicycling programs and recommending any needed changes in these programs.

D.C. Code § 50-1604 (2013). District of Columbia Bicycle Advisory Council

(a) There is established a District of Columbia Bicycle Advisory Council (the "Council").

(b)(1) The Council shall be composed of 17 members appointed as follows:

(A) The bicycle coordinator of the Office of Bicycle Transportation and Safety of the District Department of Transportation, as established in § 50-1603;

(B) The Chief of the Metropolitan Police Department or his or her designee;

(C) The Director of the Office of Planning or his or her designee;

(D) The Director of the Department of Parks and Recreation or his or her designee; and

(E) Thirteen community representatives, with each member of the Council of the District of Columbia appointing one representative.

(2)(A) Each community representative shall be a resident of the District with a demonstrated interest in bicycling.

(B) The representative appointed by the member of the Council of the District of Columbia who chairs the committee having jurisdiction over the District Department of Transportation shall serve as chairperson of the Council.

(c) The community members shall be appointed for a term of 3 years, with initial staggered appointments of 4 members appointed for 1 year, 5 members appointed for 2 years, and 4 members appointed for 3 years. The members to serve the 1-year term, the members to serve the 2-year term, and the members to serve the 3-year term shall be determined by lot at the 1st meeting of the Council.

(c-1) The District Department of Transportation shall provide the Bicycle Advisory Council with an annual operating budget, which shall include funds to maintain a website, where the Bicycle Advisory Council shall provide a public listing of members, meeting notices, and meeting minutes.

(d) The purpose of the Council shall be to serve as the advisory body to the Mayor, Council of the District of Columbia, and District agencies on matters pertaining to bicycling in the District and to make recommendations to the bicycle coordinator on the budget and focus of the Comprehensive Bicycle Transportation and Safety Program.

D.C. Code § 50-1609 (2013). Definitions

For the purposes of this subchapter the term:

(1) "Bicycle" means a human-powered vehicle with wheels designed to transport, by pedaling, one or more persons seated on one or more saddle seats on its frame. "Bicycle" also includes a human-powered vehicle, and any attachment to the vehicle designed to transport by pedaling when the vehicle is used on a public roadway, public bicycle path or other public right-of way. The term "Bicycle" also includes a "tricycle," which is a 3-wheeled human-powered vehicle designed for use as a toy by a single child under 6 years of age, the seat of which is no more than 2 feet from ground level.

(1A) "Identification number" means a numbered stamp, sticker, or other label or plate issued for a bicycle for the purpose of identifying the bicycle as having been registered, including any sticker or label provided by the National Bike Registry or a registry established by the Mayor for the purpose of bicycle registration. The term "identification number" shall also include a serial number that is originally inscribed or affixed by the manufacturer to a bicycle frame or a bicycle part for the purpose of identification.

(1B) "National Bike Registry" means the nationwide computer database for the registration of bicycles that is an official licensee of the National Crime Prevention Council and is accessible at www. nationalbikeregistry.com or at 1-800-848-BIKE.

(2) "Operator" means a person under 16 years of age who travels on a bicycle seated on a saddle seat from which that person is intended to and can pedal the bicycle.

(3) "Other public right-of-way" means any right of way other than a public roadway or public bicycle path that is under the jurisdiction and control of the District of Columbia and is designed for use and used by vehicular or pedestrian traffic.

(4) "Passenger" means any person, under 16 years of age, who travels on a bicycle in any manner except as an operator.

(5) "Protective bicycle helmet" means a piece of headgear which meets or exceeds the impact standards for protective bicycle helmets set by the American National Standards Institute (ANSI) or the Snell Memorial Foundation's standards for protective headgear or the American Society for testing and Materials (ASTM) for use in bicycling.

(6) "Public bicycle path" means a right-of-way under the jurisdiction and control of the District of Columbia for use primarily by bicycles and pedestrians.

(7) "Public roadway" means a right-of-way under the jurisdiction and control of the District of Columbia for use primarily by motor vehicles.

D.C. Code § 50-1611 (2013). Bicycle registration

(a)(1) No person shall be required to register a bicycle in the District of Columbia.

(2) A person wishing to register a bicycle to permit the Metropolitan Police Department to track or locate the bicycle if it becomes lost or stolen may do so through the National Bike Registry or a District bicycle registry established by the Mayor in accordance with this section.

(b)(1) The Mayor may establish, through rulemaking, another bicycle registry to serve as a supplement to or replacement for the National Bike Registry.

(2) Any bicycle registry established by the Mayor shall be web-based and easily utilized by any bicycle purchaser or owner, or law enforcement official.

(c)(1) Except as provided in paragraph (2) of this subsection, the Metropolitan Police Department shall check the identification number of any bicycle recovered by the Metropolitan Police Department against the National Bike Registry and any other bicycle registry established by the Mayor, and shall notify the registered owner of a recovered bicycle.

(2) If the Mayor replaces the National Bike Registry with another bicycle registry pursuant to subsection (b)(1) of this section, the Metropolitan Police Department shall be required

to check the identification number of any bicycle recovered by the Metropolitan Police only against the registry established by the Mayor.

(d) As of June 1, 2008, a person regularly engaged in the business of selling bicycles shall inform each purchaser, in writing, how to voluntarily register the purchaser's bicycle in accordance with this section. For the purposes of this subsection, the term "bicycle" shall exclude tricycles.

(e) The Mayor, pursuant to subchapter I of Chapter 5 of Title 2, may issue rules to implement the provisions of this section.

D.C. Code § 50-1612 (2013). Bicycle rental information

(a) As of June 1, 2008, a person regularly engaged in the business of renting bicycles shall require each person seeking to rent a bicycle to provide his or her signature on the rental form, or on a separate form, containing each of the following:

(1) A statement of rental bearing the names and addresses of the lessor and lessee;

(2) The rate at which the bicycle is being rented; and

(3) The time for which the bicycle is being rented.

(b) The form used to meet the requirements of subsection (a) of this section may be the same form used to meet the requirements of § 50-1605(f).

D.C. Code § 50-1621 (2013). Civil action for bicyclists

(a) An individual who, while riding a bicycle, is the victim of an assault or battery by a motorist, and prevails in a civil action for such assault or battery, shall be entitled to:

(1) Statutory damages of $1,000 or actual damages, whichever is greater;

(2) Reasonable attorney's fees and costs; provided, that the total amount of damages is less than $10,000; and

(3) Any other relief available under the law.

(b) For the purposes of this section, the term "motorist" means an individual who operates a motor vehicle, as defined in § 50-2301.02(5a).[29]

II. Helmets

D.C. Code § 50-1605 (2013). Helmet use requirements

(a) It shall be unlawful for any person under 16 years of age to operate or to be a passenger on a bicycle or any attachment to a bicycle on a public roadway, public bicycle path or other right-of-way, unless that person wears a protective helmet of good fit, fastened securely upon the head with the straps of the helmet.

(b) It shall be unlawful for any parent or legal guardian of a child under 16 years of age to knowingly permit the child to operate or to be a passenger on a bicycle on a public roadway,

---

[29] D.C. Code § 50-2301.02(5a)
The term "motor vehicle" means all vehicles propelled by an internal-combustion engine, electricity, or steam. The term "motor vehicle" shall not include traction engines, road rollers, vehicles propelled only upon stationary rails or tracks, personal mobility devices, as defined by § 50-2201.02(12), or a battery-operated wheelchair when a person with a disability.

public bicycle path, or other public right-of-way, unless at all times when the child is so engaged, he or she wears a protective bicycle helmet of good fit, fastened securely upon the head with the straps of the helmet.

(c) The parents or legal guardians of any child under 16 years of age found in violation of this section shall be liable for paying a fine of $25. However, the fine shall be suspended for:

(1) First time violators; or

(2) Violators who subsequent to the violation, but prior to the imposition of fine, purchase a helmet of the type required by this subchapter.

(d) The penalties provided for pursuant to subsection (c) of this section shall not be enforced until 90 days after May 23, 2000.

(e) Any helmet sold or rented, or offered for sale or rent, for use by operators and passengers of bicycles shall be conspicuously labeled in accordance with the standard described in § 50-1609(5).

(f)(1) A person regularly engaged in the business of renting bicycles shall require each person seeking to rent a bicycle to provide his or her signature, either on the rental form, or on a separate form containing each of the following:

(A) A written explanation of the provisions of this subchapter and the penalties for violations; and

(B) A statement concerning whether a person under 16 years of age will operate a bicycle in an area where a helmet is required.

(2) A person regularly engaged in the business of renting bicycles shall provide a properly fitted helmet to any person who will operate the bicycle in an area requiring a helmet, if the person does not already have a helmet in his or her possession. A reasonable fee may be charged for the helmet rental.

(3) A person regularly engaged in the business of selling or renting bicycles who complies with this subchapter shall not be liable in a civil action for damages for any physical injuries sustained by a bicycle operator or passenger as a result of the operator's passenger's failure to wear a helmet or to wear a properly fitted or fastened helmet in violation of this subchapter.

D.C. Code § 50-1606 (2013). Contributory negligence

Failure to wear a helmet as described in this subchapter shall not be considered as evidence of either negligence per se, contributory negligence, or assumption of the risk in any civil suit arising out of any accident in which a person under 16 years of age is injured. Failure to wear a helmet shall not be a admissible as evidence in the trial of any civil action, nor in any way diminish or reduce the damages recoverable in such action.

D.C. Code § 50-1607 (2013). Child safety helmet education program

(a) Within 60 days of May 23, 2000, the District Department of Transportation, in conjunction with the Metropolitan Police Department and District of Columbia Public Schools, shall develop and implement a public education program to educate adults and children under 16 years of age on the requirements of this subchapter and the importance of properly wearing bicycle safety helmets.

(b) By October 1, of each year, the District Department of Transportation shall provide the Council of the District of Columbia, Committee on Public Works and the Environment, or a successor committee, a report summarizing the public education activities completed during the previous fiscal year, along with any statistics collected regarding bicycle accidents and injuries during the preceding fiscal year.

D.C. Code § 50-1608 (2013). Child safety helmet assistance program

The District Department of Transportation shall adopt a helmet assistance program which shall include grants and discount programs to assist indigent parents and guardians of children under 16 years of age in obtaining safety helmets.

D.C. Code § 50-1651 (2013). Helmet requirement, miscellaneous vehicles

(a) It shall be unlawful for any person under 16 years of age to ride roller skates, a skateboard, sled, coaster, toy vehicle, sidewalk bicycle, scooter, or any similar device without wearing a protective helmet of good fit, fastened securely upon the head with the straps of the helmet.

(b) The parents or legal guardians of any child under 16 years of age found in violation of this act shall be liable for a fine of $25; provided, that the fine shall be suspended for:

(1) First time violators; or

(2) Violators who subsequent to the violation, but prior to the date the fine is due, purchase a helmet as described in subsection (a) of this section and provide proof of the purchase.

(c) Any helmet offered for sale or rent for use by an operator, or passenger, of roller-skates, a skateboard, sled, coaster, toy vehicle, sidewalk bicycle, scooter, or any similar device shall meet or exceed the impact standards for protective bicycle helmets set by the American National Standards Institute, the Snell Memorial Foundation's standards for protective headgear, or the American Society for Testing and Materials for use in bicycling.

III. Commercial Bicycle Operators

D.C. Code § 50-1631 (2013). Definitions

For purposes of this subchapter, the term:

(1) "Commercial bicycle operator" means an individual at least 16 years of age who receives financial compensation for the delivery or pick-up of goods or services by bicycle as a substantial part of his or her business or earnings, as defined by the Mayor in rules developed pursuant to § 50-1632(d)(3).

(2) "Courier company" means any firm, partnership, company, corporation, or organization operating within the District of Columbia that employs, compensates, utilizes, or contracts with a commercial bicycle operator.

(3) "Mayor" means the Mayor of the District of Columbia.

D.C. Code § 50-1632 (2013). Licensing; violations; identification numbers

(a) Except as provided in subsection (e) of this section, no commercial bicycle operator shall operate within the District of Columbia without a license issued by the Mayor. A commercial bicycle operator shall pass a bicycle safety test developed by the Mayor in order to receive a commercial bicycle operator's license.

(b) It shall be a violation of this subchapter for a commercial bicycle operator licensed under this section to:

(1) Fail to pay a license fee not to exceed $50 per year;

(2) Fail to carry a valid commercial bicycle operator's permit that shall include a photo identification listing the commercial bicycle operator's name, address, permit number, and any other information required by the Mayor pursuant to subsection (d)(3) of this section;

(3) Fail to display, in a manner visible from the rear, a valid commercial bicycle operator identification number issued by the Mayor pursuant to subsection (d)(2) of this section and, if employed by, compensated by, utilized by, or under contract to a courier company, the name and telephone number of the courier company, or if not employed by, compensated by, utilized by, or under contract to a courier company, the commercial bicycle operator's telephone number and address;

(4) Use a commercial bicycle operator's permit or identification number assigned to someone other than the commercial bicycle operator; or

(5) Violate any other requirement created by rule related to commercial bicycle operators.

(c) After notice and an opportunity to be heard, the commercial bicycle license shall not be renewed or shall be suspended or revoked upon the accumulation of a substantial number of bicycle traffic law violations and unpaid fines as determined by rules promulgated by the Mayor.

(d) The Mayor shall:

(1) Issue a commercial bicycle operator's permit to each commercial bicycle operator who has passed the required bicycle safety test and paid the license fee required under § 50-1632(b)(1);

(2) Issue commercial bicycle operator identification numbers upon request to courier companies and to commercial bicycle operators not employed by, compensated by, utilized by, or under contract to a courier company;

(3) Issue rules to implement the provisions of this subchapter pursuant to subchapter I of Chapter 5 of Title 2, within 120 days of March 29, 1988; and

(4) Develop a public education program to inform the public of the requirements of this subchapter.

(e) Commercial bicycle operators operating in the District of Columbia as of March 29, 1988 shall obtain a license from the Mayor within 180 days of March 29, 1988.

D.C. Code § 50-1633 (2013). Courier company responsibility

No courier company shall employ, compensate, utilize, or contract with a commercial bicycle operator who does not have a valid commercial bicycle operator's permit and a properly registered bicycle.

D.C. Code § 50-1634 (2013). Enforcement

(a) The Mayor shall promulgate a schedule of civil fines not to exceed $50 for violations of the provisions of this subchapter and rules promulgated pursuant to § 50-1632(d)(3).

IV. Bicycle Parking

D.C. Code § 50-1641.01 (2013). Definitions

For the purposes of this subchapter, the term "bicycle parking space" means a device or enclosure, located within a building or installation, or conveniently adjacent thereto, for securing a bicycle that is easily accessible, clearly visible and so located as to be reasonably secure from theft or vandalism.

D.C. Code § 50-1641.02 (2013). Bicycle parking space requirements

(a) A bicycle parking space shall conform to the bike parking rack standard established by the District Department of Transportation, or be of such design that will enable the frame to be supported in 2 places, and allow for both wheels of a bicycle to be secured with ease by use of a U-lock, cable lock, or other security device. Exceptions to these standards may be approved by the Mayor.

(b) Bicycle parking spaces installed prior to February 2, 2008, that do not meet the requirements of this subchapter shall be permitted until one year after February 2, 2008.

D.C. Code § 50-1641.03 (2013). John A. Wilson Building bicycle parking requirements

(a) Notwithstanding any other law or regulation, the Council shall increase the number of public bicycle parking spaces at the John A. Wilson Building.

(b) The total number of public bicycle parking spaces provided at the John A. Wilson Building shall be no less than 16; provided, that:

(1) Design, purchase, and installation of the public bicycle parking spaces shall be done in coordination with the District Department of Transportation ("DDOT") from funds either already allocated to DDOT in fiscal year 2008 or already allocated to the Council in fiscal year 2008 for the maintenance of the John A. Wilson Building;

(2) The design of the bicycle parking spaces shall be consistent with the architectural style and beauty of the John A. Wilson Building, and

(3) At least one bicycle parking space shall be located adjacent to the public entrance on Pennsylvania Avenue, N.W., if this is determined to be consistent with historic preservation guidelines and National Park Service regulations.

D.C. Code § 50-1641.04 (2013). Mayor's report on bicycle parking at District government buildings

(a) Within 180 days of February 2, 2008, the Mayor shall prepare and make public a report on the availability of bicycle parking spaces at buildings occupied by the District government, including office buildings occupied by District government agencies, public school buildings, public libraries and branches, recreation centers, and parks.

(b) The report shall include:

(1) The current number of parking spaces available for automobiles;

(2) The current number of parking spaces available for bicycles;

(3) The percentage of available bicycle parking spaces to available automobile parking spaces;

(4) A strategic plan to provide no less than a number of bicycle parking spaces that is equivalent to 10% of the available automobile parking spaces;

(5) A plan for providing a larger number of bicycle parking spaces at locations where it is warranted by current demand;

(6) An evaluation of bicycle travel lanes that lead riders to the facility or park; and

(7) A detailed report of the bicycle parking plans for the baseball stadium for the Washington Nationals.

D.C. Code § 50-1641.05 (2013). Residential building bicycle parking requirements

(a)(1) A residential building owner shall provide secure bicycle parking spaces for all existing residential buildings with 8 or more units.

(2)(A) A residential building owner shall provide a reasonable number of bicycle parking spaces, as determined by the Mayor, for all existing residential buildings within 30 days of one or more residents' written requests, unless an extension due to hardship is granted by the Mayor.

(B) Where complaints of noncompliance have been filed with the Mayor by one or more residents, the Mayor shall facilitate an agreement between the parties and determine the number of bicycle parking spaces that shall be provided.

(C) The bicycle parking spaces shall be provided within 30 days of the Mayor's determination, unless an extension due to hardship is granted by the Mayor.

(3) Where it can be demonstrated that providing bicycle parking spaces required under this subsection is not physically practical, that undue economic hardship would result from strict compliance with the regulation, or that the nature of the building use is such that bicycle parking spaces would not be used, the Mayor may grant, upon written application of the owner of the building, an appropriate exemption or reduced level of compliance. In such cases, a certificate documenting the exemption or reduced level of compliance shall be issued to the building owner.

(b)(1) A residential building owner shall provide at least one secure bicycle parking space for each 3 residential units for all new residential buildings and substantially rehabilitated buildings with 8 or more units.

(2) Where it can be demonstrated in a substantially rehabilitated building that providing bicycle parking spaces is not physically practical, that undue economic hardship would result from strict compliance with the regulation, or that the nature of the building use is such that bicycle parking would

not be used, the Mayor may grant, upon written application of the owner of the building, an appropriate exemption or reduced level of compliance. In such cases, a certificate documenting the exemption or reduced level of compliance shall be issued to the building owner.

(3) For the purposes of this subsection, "substantially rehabilitated" means any improvement to or renovation of a residential building for which the improvement or renovation equals or exceeds 50% of the assessed value of the building before the rehabilitation. Existing bicycle parking spaces before rehabilitation shall be considered in calculating the total number of required parking spaces under this subsection.

(c) The Mayor shall identify categories that are eligible for appropriate exemption or reduced level of compliance. The categories include "elderly housing", "assisted living facilities", and "nursing homes" as defined in § 44-501.

(d) Any residential buildings that have been exempted from the regulation due to the nature of the use of the building shall provide a minimum number of bicycle parking spaces equal to at least 5% of the number of people employed at the building.

D.C. Code § 50-1641.06 (2013). Increased bicycle parking spaces for office, retail, and service uses

(a) An owner of a building with office, retail, or service use shall provide a minimum number of bicycle parking spaces at least equal to 5% of the number of automobile parking spaces provided for the building.

(b) If the utilization of the minimum number of bicycle parking spaces is reaching 90% or higher during peak usage periods, the owner of a building with office, retail, or service use shall provide bicycle parking spaces at least equal to 10% of the number of automobile parking spaces provided for the building.

(c) Where it can be demonstrated that providing bicycle parking spaces is not physically practical, that undue economic hardship would result from strict compliance with the regulation, or that the nature of the building use is such that bicycle parking spaces would not be used, the Mayor may grant, upon written application of the owner of the building, an appropriate exemption or reduced level of compliance. In such cases, a certificate documenting the exemption or reduced level of compliance shall be issued to the building owner.

D.C. Code § 50-1641.07a (2013). Enforcement

(a) A violation of this subchapter or the rules issued under authority of this subchapter shall be a civil infraction for the purposes of Chapter 18 of Title 2.

(b) Civil fines, penalties, and fees may be imposed as sanctions for an infraction of § 50-1641.05 or § 50-1641.06, or any rule promulgated under authority of this subchapter, pursuant to Chapter 18 of Title 2.

(c) Six months after April 8, 2001, the Mayor may begin enforcement of § 50-1641.06(a).

(d) Six months after the effective date of the rules issued

pursuant to § 50-1641.07, the Mayor may begin enforcement of § 50-1641.05 and § 50-1641.06(b) and (c).

(e) Revenues collected from enforcement described in subsections (c) and (d) of this section shall be dedicated to any costs associated with conducting such enforcement. (a) A violation of this subchapter or the rules issued under authority of this subchapter shall be a civil infraction for the purposes of Chapter 18 of Title 2.

TITLE 50. MOTOR AND NON-MOTOR VEHICLES
AND TRAFFIC (cont'd)
SUBTITLE VII. TRAFFIC

D.C. Code § 50-2201.28 (2013). Right-of-way at crosswalks

(b-1) A person on a bicycle or operating a personal mobility device upon or along a sidewalk or while crossing a roadway in a crosswalk shall have the rights and duties applicable to a pedestrian under the same circumstances;[30] provided, that:

(1) The bicyclist or personal mobility device operator yields to pedestrians on the sidewalk or crosswalk; and

(2) Riding a bicycle on the sidewalk is permitted.

D.C. Code § 50-2201.32 (2013). Speed limit assessment

(a) By November 1, 2013, the Mayor shall complete a District-wide assessment that evaluates the speed limits on the District's arterials and other streets. The report of the assessment shall include the criteria used for assessing the speed limits. Upon its completion, the assessment shall be posted to the District Department of Transportation's website. The assessment shall identify a list of recommended speed limits for all District streets based on each of the following independent approaches:

---

[30] Specifically:

(a) The driver of a vehicle shall stop and remain stopped to allow a pedestrian to cross the roadway within any marked crosswalk, or unmarked crosswalk at an intersection, when the pedestrian is upon the lane, or within one lane approaching the lane, on which the vehicle is traveling or onto which it is turning.

(a-1) Whenever a vehicle is stopped at a marked crosswalk at an unsignalized intersection, a vehicle approaching the crosswalk in an adjacent lane or from behind the stopped vehicle shall stop and give the right-of-way to ensure the safety of pedestrians and bicyclists before passing the stopped vehicle.

(b) A pedestrian who has begun crossing on the "WALK" signal shall be given the right-of-way by the driver of any vehicle to continue to the opposite sidewalk or safety island, whichever is nearest.

(2) Use factors based on safety and mobility needs of pedestrians, bicyclists, transit drivers and all other potential road users, as well as factors based on input from local neighborhood representatives and organizations that promote road safety including . . . the Bicycle Advisory Council.

D.C. Code § 50-2302.02 (2013). Exceptions [Moving infractions]

The provisions of this subchapter shall not apply to the following violations, which shall continue to be prosecuted as criminal offenses:

(13) Violation of § 11.701(a) of Title 32 of the District of Columbia Rules and Regulations (tampering with a locked or secured bicycle).

TITLE 50. MOTOR AND NON-MOTOR VEHICLES AND TRAFFIC (cont'd)
MISC. PROVISIONS

D.C. Code § 50-205 (2013). Bicycle safety enhancements for District-owned, heavy-duty vehicles

(a) The Mayor shall:

(1) Equip all District-owned, heavy-duty vehicles with the following:

(A) Blind-spot mirrors;

(B) Reflective blind-spot warning stickers;

(2) Require that operators of District-owned, heavy-duty

vehicles receive bicycle and pedestrian safety training from a curriculum and instructors that are approved by the District Department of Transportation.

D.C. Code § 50-921.04 (2013). Duties [Dept. of Transportation]

The offices of the DDOT shall plan, program, operate, manage, control, and maintain systems, processes, and programs to meet transportation needs as follows:

(1) Infrastructure Project Management Administration shall:

(B) Manage and construct capital projects related to the design and installation of streets, alleys, curbs, gutters, bicycle lanes, sidewalks, streetscapes, and medians;

(K) Develop policies and programs to encourage and provide for the safe use of bicycles for recreation and work-related travel, including planning, developing, operating, and regulating a Bike Sharing program, and administering the Bicycle Sharing Fund established by § 50-921.16 to fund a Bike Sharing program.

(3) Traffic Services Administration shall:

(B) Incorporate transportation safety features in the development, design, and construction of pedestrian, bicycle, motor vehicle, and mass transportation facilities and programs.

D.C. Code § 50-921.16 (2013). Bicycle Sharing Fund

(a) There is established as a nonlapsing, special purpose

revenue fund the Bicycle Sharing Fund ("Fund"). The fund shall be administered by the Director of the District Department of Transportation and used to pay for goods, services, property and for any other purpose under the Bike Sharing program established pursuant to § 50-921.04(2)(K).

(b) All revenue related to the Bike Sharing program, from whatever source derived, shall be deposited into the Fund as of March 19, 2013.

(c) All funds deposited into the Fund, including any interest earned on those funds, shall not revert to the unrestricted fund balance of the General Fund of the District of Columbia at the end of a fiscal year, or at any other time, but shall be continually available for the uses and purposes set forth in subsection (a) of this section without regard to fiscal year limitation, subject to authorization by Congress.

D.C. Code § 50-2534 (2013). Expenditure of Performance Parking Pilot Program revenue

(b) The Mayor shall involve performance parking pilot zone residents, businesses, ANCs, and Ward Councilmembers in prioritizing non-automobile transportation improvements. The improvements may include:

(3) Improvements to bicycling infrastructure, such as painted and separated bicycle lanes, installation of public bicycle racks, and way-finding signage for bicyclists.

MISC. PROVISIONS (OTHER)

D.C. Code § 1-325.131 (2013). Pedestrian and Bicycle Safety and Enhancement Fund

(a) There is established as a nonlapsing fund the Pedestrian and Bicycle Safety and Enhancement Fund ("Fund"), which shall be allocated $1.5 million per fiscal year from the fines generated from the enhanced neighborhood parking control initiative. . . .

(b)(1) The Fund shall be used solely to enhance the safety and quality of pedestrian and bicycle transportation, including traffic calming and Safe Routes to School enhancements. . . .

D.C. Code § 22-2302 (2013). Prohibited acts [panhandling]

(g) No person may ask, beg, or solicit alms in exchange for protecting, watching, washing, cleaning, repairing, or painting a motor vehicle or bicycle while it is parked on a public street.

D.C. Code § 22-3234 (2013). Altering or removing bicycle identification numbers

(a) It is unlawful for a person to knowingly remove, obliterate, tamper with, or alter any identification number on a bicycle or bicycle part.

(b) Any person who violates subsection (a) of this section shall be guilty of a misdemeanor and, upon conviction, shall be imprisoned for not more than 180 days, or fined not more than $1,000, or both.

(c) For the purposes of this section, the term:

(1) "Bicycle" shall have the same meaning as provided in § 50-1609(1).

(2) "Identification number" shall have the same meaning as provided in § 50-1609(1A).

D.C. Code § 31-2403.01 (2013). Pre-litigation discovery of insurance[31]

(a) After a claimant makes a written claim for compensation or damages concerning a vehicle accident, and provides the documents described in subsection (b) or (c) of this section to an insurer, the claimant shall be entitled to obtain from the insurer documentation of the applicable limits of coverage in any insurance agreement under which the insurer may be liable to:

(1) Satisfy all or part of the claim; or

(2) Indemnify or reimburse for payments made to satisfy the claim.

(b) For a claimant to obtain the documentation described in subsection (a) of this section from the insurer, the claimant shall provide the following, in writing, to the insurer:

(1) The date of the vehicle accident;

(2) The name and last known address of the alleged tortfeasor;

(3) A copy of the vehicle accident report, if any;

[31] This provision is applicable to accidents involving bicycles (see paragraph (h).

(4) The insurer's claim number, if available;

(5) The claimant's health care bills and documentation of the claimant's loss of income, if any, resulting from the vehicle accident; and

(6) The records of health care treatment for the claimant's injuries caused by the vehicle accident.

(c) If the claim is brought by the estate of an individual or a beneficiary of the individual, whose death resulted from a vehicle accident, the insurer must provide the documentation described in subsection (a) of this section if the claimant provides the following, in writing, to the insurer:

(1) The date of the vehicle accident;

(2) The name and last known address of the alleged tortfeasor;

(3) A copy of the vehicle accident report, if any;

(4) The insurer's claim number, if available;

(5) A copy of the decedent's death certificate issued in the District of Columbia or another jurisdiction;

(6) A copy of the letters of administration issued to appoint the personal representative of the decedent's estate in the District of Columbia or a substantially similar document issued by another jurisdiction;

(7) The name of each beneficiary of the decedent, if known;

(8) The relationship to the decedent of each known beneficiary of the decedent;

(9) The health care bills for health care treatment, if any, of the decedent resulting from the vehicle accident; and

(10) The records of health care treatment for injuries to the decedent caused by the vehicle accident.

(d) After receipt of the documents pursuant to either subsection (b) or (c) of this section, the insurer shall respond in writing within 30 days of receipt of the request issued pursuant to subsection (a) of this section and shall disclose the limits of coverage, of all policies, regardless of whether the insurer contests the applicability of the policy to the claim.

(e) Disclosure of documentation required under this section shall not constitute:

(1) An admission that the asserted claim is subject to the applicable agreement between the insurer and the alleged tortfeasor; or

(2) A waiver of any term or condition of the applicable agreement between the insurer and the alleged tortfeasor or any right of the insurer, including any potential defense concerning coverage or liability.

(f) An insurer, and the employees and agents of an insurer, may not be civilly or criminally liable for disclosure of the required documentation.

(g) Information concerning the insurance policy is not, by reason of disclosure pursuant to this section, admissible as evidence at trial.

(h) For the purposes of this section, the term "vehicle accident" includes accidents involving bicyclists.

(Emphasis added)

D.C. Code § 35-251 (2013). Unlawful conduct on public passenger vehicles

(b) It is unlawful for any person either while aboard a public passenger vehicle with a capacity for seating 12 or more passengers, including vehicles owned and/or operated by the Washington Metropolitan Area Transit Authority, which is transporting passengers in regular route service within the corporate limits of the District of Columbia; or while aboard a rail transit car owned and/or operated by the Washington Metropolitan Area Transit Authority which is transporting passengers within the corporate limits of the District of Columbia; or while within a rail transit station owned and/or operated by the Washington Metropolitan Area Transit Authority which is located within the corporate limits of the District of Columbia to:

(10) Park, operate, carry, wheel, or chain to any fence, tree, railing, or other structure not specifically designated for such use, noncollapsible bicycles, unless an individual has a current permit issued by the Washington Metropolitan Area Transit Authority for the transporting of noncollapsible bicycles by rail transit and the individual is complying with all the terms and conditions of said permit; provided, that an individual shall surrender said permit upon the request or demand of any agent or employee of the Washington Metropolitan Area

Transit Authority. Sections 35-252 and 35-253 shall not apply to a violation of the terms and conditions of said permit.

D.C. Code § 38-3101 (2013). Installation of traffic control devices

(a) The Mayor shall install traffic control devices, as deemed necessary, after completing an investigation of school zones.

(b) The Mayor shall, when conducting an investigation, consider the number of persons who have been struck by a vehicle, bicycle, or motorcycle in a school zone, the likelihood of these accidents occurring in the future and the volume of traffic.

(c) The District of Columbia Public Schools and the Metropolitan Police Department shall submit monthly statistical reports to the Mayor which shall include:

(1) The number of persons who were hit by a vehicle, bicycle or motorcycle in and around school zones; and

(2) The type of injuries suffered.

D.C. Code § 47-2853.04 (2013). Regulated non-health related occupations and professions

(a) The following non-health related occupations and professions have been determined to require regulation in order to protect public health, safety or welfare, or to assure the public that persons engaged in such occupations or professions have the specialized skills or training required to perform the services offered:

(11) Commercial Bicycle Operator

(c) All non-health related occupations and professions shall be regulated by the Mayor through the Department of Consumer and Regulatory Affairs, except as follows:

(6) Commercial drivers and commercial bicycle operators shall be regulated by the Department of Public Works, as provided in Chapter 16 of Title 50 and Chapter 4 of Title 50.

APPENDIX 2(A)
DISTRICT OF COLUMBIA MUNICIPAL REGULATIONS
D.C. MUNICIPAL REGULATIONS (DCMR)
TITLE 18. VEHICLES AND TRAFFIC
CHAPTER 12. BICYCLES, MOTORIZED BICYCLES, AND MISCELLANEOUS VEHICLES

18 DCMR § 1200. Bicycles, motorized bicycles, and personal mobility devices: general provisions

(1200.1) This chapter shall apply to all bicycles operated upon all public space in the District of Columbia.

(1200.2) No person may own or operate a bicycle in the District except in accordance with the provisions of this chapter.

(1200.3) Operators of bicycles have the same rights as do operators of other vehicles and in the additional rights granted by this chapter.

(1200.4) No operator's permit shall be required for the operation of a bicycle or personal mobility device.

(1200.5) No person shall be subject to the loss or suspension of his or her motor vehicle operator's permit for violation of any regulation under this chapter.

(1200.6) No points shall accrue toward the loss of or suspension of a motor vehicle operator's permit by reason of a violation committed while operating a bicycle, sidewalk bicycle, or a personal mobility device.

(1200.7) [REPEALED]

(1200.8) No person, except for impoundment by the Mayor, shall tamper with any bicycle or personal mobility device that has been locked, placed in a rack, or otherwise secured. Any person found tampering with any bicycle or personal mobility device may be required to pay a fine of $100.

(1200.9) No person shall remove from a place of storage, possess, convey, transfer, buy, sell, lend, or rent any bicycle except as provided in this chapter.

(1200.10) No motorized bicycle shall be operated upon any public space in the District by any person who is less than sixteen (16) years old.

18 DCMR § 1201. Safe operation of bicycles and motorized bicycles

(1201.1) Every person who propels a vehicle by human power or rides a bicycle on a highway shall have the same duties as any other vehicle operator under this title, except as otherwise expressly provided in this chapter, and except for those duties imposed by this title which, by their nature or wording, can have no reasonable application to a bicycle operator.

(1201.2) A person shall operate a bicycle, sidewalk bicycle or personal mobility device in a safe and non-hazardous manner so as not to endanger himself or herself or any other person.

(1201.3)(a) A person operating a bicycle may overtake and pass another vehicle only under conditions which permit the movement to be made with safety.

(b) A person operating a bicycle may overtake and pass other vehicles on the left or right side, staying in the same lane as the overtaken vehicle, or changing to a different lane, or riding off the roadway, as necessary to pass with safety.

(c) If a lane is partially occupied by vehicles that are stopped, standing, or parked in that lane, a person operating a bicycle may ride in that or in the next adjacent lane used by vehicles proceedings in the same direction.

(1201.4) No person shall operate or ride a bicycle other than upon or astride a regular seat attached to the bicycle.

(1201.5) No person shall operate or ride on a bicycle with more persons on it at any one time than the bicycle is equipped to carry.

(1201.6) No person shall operate or ride a bicycle while carrying any package, bundle, or article which prevents the operator from keeping at least one hand on the handle bars.

(1201.7) Persons riding upon a roadway shall not ride more than two abreast except on paths or part of roadways set aside for the exclusive use of bicycles. Persons riding two abreast shall not impede the normal and reasonable movement of traffic and, on a lane roadway, shall ride within a single lane.

(1201.8) No person shall operate a bicycle at a speed in excess of any posted limit or at a speed which is greater than is reasonable and prudent under the conditions then existing.

(1201.9) There shall be no prohibition against any person riding a bicycle or personal mobility device upon a sidewalk within the District, so long as the rider does not create a hazard; provided, that no person shall ride a bicycle or operate a personal mobility device upon a sidewalk within the Central Business District except on those sidewalks expressly designated by Order of the Mayor, nor shall any person ride a bicycle upon a sidewalk in any area outside of the Central Business District if it is expressly prohibited by Order of the Mayor and appropriate signs to such effect are posted.

(1201.10) Any person riding a bicycle or personal mobility device upon a sidewalk shall yield the right-of-way to pedestrians, and shall travel at a speed no greater than the posted speed limit of the adjacent roadway; provided, that such speed is safe for the conditions then existing on the sidewalk.

(1201.11) A person propelling a bicycle or operating a personal mobility device upon and along a sidewalk or while crossing a roadway in a crosswalk shall have all the rights and duties applicable to a pedestrian under the same circumstances, except that the bicyclist or personal mobility device operator must yield to pedestrians on the sidewalk or crosswalk.

(1201.12) The operator of a bicycle or personal mobility device emerging from, or entering an alley, driveway, or building, shall upon approaching a sidewalk, or the sidewalk area extending across any alleyway, yield the right-of-way to all pedestrians approaching on said sidewalk, and upon entering the roadway shall yield the right-of-way to all vehicles approaching on said roadway, to the extent necessary to safely enter the flow of traffic.

(1201.13) No bicyclist shall suddenly leave a sidewalk and ride into the path of a vehicle which is so close that it is impossible for the driver to yield.

(1201.14) No person operating a bicycle shall sound any warning device at any intersection so as to interfere with the obedience to the instructions of official traffic control signals or to the directions of police traffic control officers.

(1201.15) No person shall operate a bicycle except in obedience to the instructions of official traffic control signals, signs, and other control devices applicable to vehicles, unless otherwise directed by a police officer or other person authorized to direct and control traffic.

(1201.16) No person riding upon a bicycle shall attach himself or herself or the device upon which he or she is riding to any vehicle upon a highway, roadway, or in an alley.

(1201.17) All provisions of this section shall be equally applicable to the operation and riding of motorized bicycles, except as specifically provided in this chapter; provided, that nothing in this chapter shall be construed as to limit the applicability of Chapters 1, 4, 5, 6, and 7 with respect to the licensing, registration, inspection, or equipment of motorized bicycles or motorcycles.

(1201.18) Except as otherwise permitted for a motor vehicle, no person shall operate a motorized bicycle on any sidewalk or any off-street bikepath or bicycle route within the District. This prohibition shall apply even though the motorized bicycle is being operated solely by human power.

(1201.19) A motorized bicycle may be operated on any part of a roadway designated for the use of bicycles.

18 DCMR § 1204. Bicycle safety equipment

(1204.1) Each bicycle shall be equipped with a brake which enables the operator to cause the braked wheels to skid on dry, level, clean pavement; provided, that a fixed gear bicycle is not required to have a separate brake, but an operator of a fixed gear bicycle shall be able to stop the bicycle using the pedals.

(1204.2) Each bicycle, when in use at night, shall be equipped with a lamp on the front which shall emit a steady or flashing white light visible from a distance of at least five hundred feet (500 ft.) to the front and with a red reflector on the rear which shall be visible from all distances from fifty feet (50 ft.) to three hundred feet (300 ft.) to the rear when directly in front of upper beams of head lamps on a motor vehicle.

(1204.3) A lamp emitting a steady or flashing red light visible from a distance of five hundred feet (500 ft.) to the rear may be used in lieu of the red reflector.

(1204.4) In place of the requirements of § 1204.2, a lamp may be worn on the body of an operator; provided, that it may be readily seen from the distances set forth in that subsection.

(1204.5) Each bicycle shall be equipped with a bell or other device capable of giving a signal audible for a distance of at least one hundred feet (100 ft.).

(1204.6) A bicycle shall not be equipped with, nor shall any bicycle rider use, a siren of any kind.

(1204.7) A bicycle rider shall not use the device for giving an audible signal when operating the bicycle within the quiet zone established by the provisions of D.C. Law 2-53 within one hundred (100) yards of any school, college, or university while classes are in session, or within one hundred (100) yards of any hospital or institution for the treatment of sick persons, except where such use is reasonably necessary for the safety of the rider or pedestrians.

18 DCMR § 1206. Transporting bicycles

(1206.1) A mountable rack may be attached to a vehicle for the purpose of transporting a bicycle; Provided, that the number of bicycles transported in the rack shall not exceed the number which the rack is designed to carry.

(1206.2) No mountable rack shall extend beyond the bumper design margins of a vehicle in any manner which is hazardous or dangerous, nor shall any such mountable rack obstruct the vehicle's stop or turn signals.

18 DCMR § 1207. Sale and rental of bicycles

(1207.1) Every person engaged in the business of buying or selling bicycles shall inform a purchaser of the purpose and procedure for registration of bicycles.

(1207.2) - (1207.3) [REPEALED]

(1207.4) Every person who sells or transfers a new bicycle to any other person within the District shall, within four (4) business days after the sale or transfer, deliver to the transferee a certificate of sale properly describing and identifying the bicycle.

(1207.5) - (1207.7) [REPEALED]

(1207.8) Every person engaged in the business of renting bicycles shall issue to each person who rents a bicycle a statement of rental bearing the names and addresses of the lessor and lessee, the rate at which the bicycle is rented, and the time for which it is rented.

(1207.9) It shall be the duty of the owner, proprietor, or person in charge of any store or shop where bicycles, motor bicycles, tricycles, or similar vehicles are left for repair, to keep a written record of the number and make of each vehicle so left, together with the name and residence of the owner of the vehicle and the name and residence of the person leaving the vehicle at the store or shop.

18 DCMR § 1208. Bicycle racks

(1208.1) No bicycle rack shall be placed on public space unless a permit has been obtained from the Mayor.

(1208.2) [REPEALED]

(1208.3) No permit shall be issued for any rack which would unduly obstruct pedestrian movement.

(1208.4) There shall be no fee for rental of public space for racks.

(1208.5) Any rack placed on public space by the permittee shall be removable; shall be maintained in a good, clean condition; and shall not be allowed to deteriorate, become unsightly, or dangerous to the public.

18 DCMR § 1209. Parking bicycles on public space

(1209.1) A person may secure a bicycle to a stanchion for a period of not more than twelve (12) consecutive hours, by means of a lock or similar device, in accordance with the requirements of § 1209.2.

(1209.2) A person may secure a bicycle to a stanchion by means of a lock or similar device as long as securing the bicycle does not obstruct or unduly impede traffic or pedestrian movement and as long as securing bicycles has not been forbidden by any notice posted by the Director.

(1209.3) No person shall secure a bicycle to any of the following publicly-owned facilities:

(a) Fire hydrants;

(b) Police and fire call boxes;

(c) Electric traffic signal poles;

(d) Stanchions or poles located within bus zones or stands;

(e) Stanchions or poles located within twenty-five feet (25 ft.) of an intersection;

(f) Trees under ten inches (10 in.) in diameter.

(1209.4) There shall be no fee charged for use of parking meter stanchions used in accordance with these regulations; Provided, that the parking space adjacent to the meter is not occupied by the bicycle.

(1209.5) The Director may remove any bicycle secured to a stanchion which is not in compliance with this section; Provided, that the bicycle is impounded in accordance with the provisions of this chapter.

(1209.6) Except as provided in this chapter, no person shall park a bicycle:

(a) Upon a highway other than the roadway against the curb; or

(b) Upon a sidewalk; except in a rack to support the bicycle, against a building, or at the curb in such a manner as to afford the least obstruction to pedestrian traffic.

(1209.7) All provisions of this section shall be equally applicable to the parking or securing of motorized bicycles.

18 DCMR § 1210. Removal of bicycles from public space

(1210.1) Any bicycle left unused in public space for more than thirty (30) days shall be considered abandoned. The Director may remove an abandoned bicycle after placing notice on the bicycle for a period of at least ten (10) days. The Director shall attempt to identify and contact the owner of a registered bicycle prior to removing it from public space.

(1210.2) Bicycles removed from public space that are in working order may be auctioned off to the highest bidder or given free-of-charge to minors as part of a bicycle recreation, safety, or responsibility program. Bicycles that are not in working order may be disposed of as solid waste.

18 DCMR § 1211. Operation of miscellaneous vehicles

(1211.1) No person . . . riding by means of a . . . sidewalk bicycle . . . shall go upon any roadway except when crossing a roadway in a crosswalk. When crossing a roadway, such person shall be granted all the rights and shall be subject to all the duties applicable to pedestrians. This subsection shall not apply to any street set aside as a play street by the Mayor or the Council.

(1211.2) No person riding upon a . . . sidewalk bicycle . . . shall attach himself or herself or the device upon which he or she is riding to any vehicle upon a highway, roadway, or in an alley.

18 DCMR § 1213. Pedicabs

(1213.1) Pedicabs shall be operated in accordance with the safe operation of bicycle regulations set forth in § 1201.

(1213.2) Notwithstanding § 1213.1, pedicabs shall be operated only on public streets.

(1213.3) Each pedicab shall meet the following safety requirements:

(a) The maximum width of the pedicab shall be fifty-five inches (55 in.);

(b) The maximum length of the pedicab shall be ten feet (10 ft.);

(c) The pedicab shall be equipped with:

(1) Passenger seat belts (either one (1) seat belt for each passenger or one (1) seat belt that covers all passengers);

(2) Hydraulic or mechanical disc or drum brakes, which shall be unaffected by rain or wet conditions;

(3) At least one (1) and no more than two (2) battery-operated head lamps capable of projecting a beam of white light for a distance of three hundred feet (300 ft.) in front of the pedicab, under normal atmospheric conditions at the times that use of the head lamp is required;

(4) Battery-operated tail lamps mounted on the rear of the pedicab, which, when operated, shall emit a red beam of light visible from a distance of five hundred feet (500 ft.) to the rear, under normal atmospheric conditions at the times that use of the head lamp is required;

(5) Turn lights;

(6) A bell or other device capable of giving a signal audible for a distance of at least one hundred feet (100 ft.); and

(7) Reflectors on the spokes of the wheels of the pedicab.

(d) Reflective tape that meets the following requirements shall be affixed on the side and back of the pedicab:

(1) The tape shall be at least two inches (2 in.) wide;

(2) The tape shall be at least twelve inches (12 in.) long; and

(3) There shall be at least two (2) pieces of tape on each side and on the back of the pedicab.

(1213.4) Each pedicab shall be operated in accordance with the following provisions:

(a) The maximum number of passengers a pedicab may transport shall not exceed the number of available seats;

(b) All passengers shall be seated while the pedicab is in motion;

(c) All passengers shall have a seatbelt securely fastened while the pedicab is in motion. This requirement shall be clearly displayed to pedicab passengers;

(d) A pedicab shall not be operated on a roadway with a posted speed limit of more than thirty miles per hour (30 mph);

(e) A pedicab may not be operated or parked on a sidewalk;

(f) Pedicab passengers shall be loaded and off-loaded while the pedicab is stopped;

(g) No pedicab operator shall stop to load or unload passengers on the traffic side of the street, while occupying any intersection or crosswalk, or in such a manner as to unduly interfere with the orderly flow of traffic. All pedicab operators shall pull as close to the curb or edge of the roadway as possible to take on or discharge passengers;

(h) A pedicab shall not be parked in any restricted zones identified for other vehicles, including, but not limited to, parking meter zones, residential permit parking zones, valet parking zones, bus zones, taxicab zones;

(i) A pedicab shall not be tied, cabled, or otherwise attached to a parking meter, street light pole, or other public space asset;

(j) At any time from one half (1/2) hour after sunset to one-half (1/2) hour before sunrise, and at any other time when, due to insufficient light or unfavorable atmospheric conditions, persons and vehicles on the highway are not clearly discernible at a distance of five hundred feet (500 ft.) ahead, a pedicab shall be operated with a headlamp of sufficient intensity to reveal a person or a vehicle three hundred feet (300 ft.); and

(k) At any time from one half (1/2) hour after sunset to one-half (1/2) hour before sunrise, and at any other time when, due to insufficient light or unfavorable atmospheric conditions, persons and vehicles on the highway are not clearly discernible at a distance of five hundred feet (500 ft.) ahead, a pedicab shall be operated with tail lamps capable of being seen from a distance of five hundred feet (500 ft.).

(1213.5) No one shall operate or be in control of a pedicab while the person's alcohol concentration is eight hundredths of a gram (0.08 g.) or more either per one hundred milliliters (100 ml.) of blood or per two hundred and ten liters (210 L.) of breath or is one tenth of a gram (0.10 g.) or more per one hundred milliliters (100 ml.) of urine, or while under the influence of intoxicating liquor or any drug or any combination thereof, or while the ability to operate a vehicle is impaired by the consumption of intoxicating liquor.

TITLE 18. VEHICLES AND TRAFFIC (cont'd)
CHAPTER 7. MOTOR VEHICLE EQUIPMENT

18 DCMR § 704. Headlamps

(704.3) Each . . . motorized bicycle shall be equipped with at least one (1) and not more than two (2) head lamps which shall comply with the requirements and limitations of this chapter.

(704.4) Each head lamp on each motor vehicle, including each . . . motorized bicycle, shall be located at a height measured from the center of the head lamp of not more than fifty-four inches (54 in.) or less than twenty-four inches (24 in.) to be measured from the center of the lamp or device to the level ground on which the vehicle stands when the vehicle is without a load.

18 DCMR § 706. Stop lamps, turn signals, and reflectors

(706.2) [M]otorized bicycles shall be equipped with at least one (1) stop lamp meeting the requirements of § 713.

(706.4) [M]otorized bicycles . . . shall be exempt from the requirements of § 706.3.[32]

(706.6) [E]ach . . . motorized bicycle shall carry at least one (1) reflector meeting the requirements of this section. . . .

(706.7) Each reflector shall be mounted on the vehicle at a height not less than fifteen inches (15 in.) or more than sixty

[32] (706.3) No motor vehicle, trailer, or semi-trailer, manufactured or assembled on and after September 15, 1955, shall be operated in the District unless it is equipped with electric turn signals meeting the requirements of § 713.

inches (60 in.) measured as set forth in § 703.3, and shall be of such size and characteristics and so mounted as to be visible at night from all distances within three hundred feet (300 ft.) to fifty feet (50 ft.) from the vehicle when directly in front of lawful upperbeams of head lamps, except that visibility from a greater distance is required of reflectors on certain types of vehicles.

18 DCMR § 713. Signal lamps and signal devices

(713.2) Stop lamps on motor-driven cycles and motorized bicycles may be actuated upon application of the left handlebar brake.

(713.4) When lamps are used for turn indicators, the lamps showing to the front shall be located on the same level and as widely spaced laterally as practicable, and when in use shall display a white or amber light, or any shade of color between white and amber, visible from a distance of not less than one hundred feet (100 ft.) to the front in normal sunlight. The lamps showing to the rear shall be located at the same level and as widely spaced laterally as practicable, and when in use shall display a red or amber light, or any shade of color between red and amber, visible from a distance of not less than one hundred feet (100 ft.) to the rear in normal sunlight.

(713.5) When actuated, turn indicator lamps shall indicate the direction of the intended turn by flashing the light showing to the front and rear on the side toward which the turn is going to be made.

(713.6) No stop lamp or signal lamp shall project a glaring light.

18 DCMR § 717. Lighting equipment on motor-driven cycles and motorized bicycles

(717.1) The headlamp or headlamps on each motor-driven cycle or motorized bicycle, whether of the single-beam or multiple-beam type, shall comply with the requirements and limitations of this section.

(717.2) Each headlamp on a motor-driven cycle or motorized bicycle shall be of sufficient intensity to reveal a person or a vehicle as follows:

(a) At a distance of not less than one hundred feet (100 ft.) when the motor-driven cycle or motorized bicycle is operated at any speed less than twenty-five miles per hour (25 mph);

(b) At a distance of not less than two hundred feet (200 ft.) when the motor-driven cycle or motorized bicycle is operated at a speed of twenty-five miles per hour (25 mph) or more; and

(c) At a distance of not less than three hundred feet (300 ft.) when the motor-driven cycle or motorized bicycle is operated at a speed of thirty-five miles per hour (35 mph) or more.

(717.3) If a motor-driven cycle or motorized bicycle is equipped with a multiple-beam headlamp or headlamps, it shall meet the following requirements:

(a) The upper beam shall meet the minimum requirements of § 717.2 and shall not exceed the limitations set forth in § 715[33]; and

(b) The lowermost beam shall meet the requirements applicable to a lowermost distribution of light as set forth in § 715.

(717.4) If a motor-driven cycle or motorized bicycle is equipped with a single-beam lamp or lamps, the lamp(s) shall be so aimed that when the vehicle is loaded none of the high-

[33] 18 DCMR 715. Multiple-beam road lighting equipment

(715.1) Except as provided otherwise in this section, the headlamps, the auxiliary driving lamp, the auxiliary passing lamp, or combination of such lamps on motor vehicles other than motorcycles or motorized bicycles shall be so arranged that the driver may select at will between distributions of light projected to different elevations. These lamps may be so arranged that the selection can be made automatically, subject to the limitations stated in this section.

(715.2) There shall be an uppermost distribution of light, or composite beam, so aimed and of such intensity as to reveal persons and vehicles at a distance of at least three hundred fifty feet (350 ft.) ahead for all conditions of loading.

(715.3) There shall be a lowermost distribution of light, or composite beam, so aimed and of sufficient intensity to reveal persons and vehicles at a distance of least one hundred feet (100 ft.) ahead; and on a straight, level road under any condition of loading, none of the high-intensity portion of the beam shall be directed to strike the eyes of an approaching driver.

(715.4) Each new motor vehicle, other than a motorcycle or motorized bicycle, which has multiple-beam road lighting equipment shall be equipped with a beam indicator, which shall be lighted whenever the uppermost distribution of light from the head lamps is in use, and shall not otherwise be lighted. This indicator shall be so designed and located that when lighted it will be readily visible without glare to the driver of the vehicle so equipped.

(715.5) Each motor vehicle equipped with multiple-beam head lamps operating on the highways of the District when lights are required shall use the lower or city-driving beam.

intensity portion of light, at a distance of twenty-five feet (25 ft.) ahead shall project higher than the level of the center of the lamp from which it comes.

(717.5) Each motor-driven cycle and motorized bicycle equipped with multiple-beam headlamp(s) operating on the highways of the District when lights are required shall use the lower or city driving beam.

18 DCMR § 720. Brakes: General provisions

(720.9) Each vehicle shall be equipped with brakes acting on all wheels except the following vehicles:

(e) The wheel of a sidecar attached to a . . . motorized bicycle, or the front wheel of a motorized bicycle need not be equipped with brakes, [provided that] the . . . motorized bicycle is capable of complying with the performance requirements of § 724. . . .

(720.13) The Director is authorized to require an inspection of the braking system on any motorized bicycle and to disapprove any braking system on a vehicle which he or she finds will not comply with the performance ability standard set forth in § 724 or which, in his or her opinion, is equipped with a braking system that is not so designed or constructed as to ensure reasonable and reliable performance in actual use.

(720.14) The Director may refuse to register or may suspend or revoke the registration of any vehicle referred to in this section when he or she determines that the braking system on the vehicle does not comply with the provisions of §§ 720 through 725.

(720.15) No person shall operate on any street or highway any vehicle referred to in this section if the Director has disapproved the braking system upon the vehicle.

18 DCMR § 730. Horns and warning devices

(730.4) No vehicle, other than an authorized emergency vehicle as set forth in § 712, shall be equipped with nor shall any person use upon a vehicle any siren, whistle, or bell, except as otherwise permitted in this chapter.

(730.5) The prohibition in § 730.4 relating to the use of a bell shall not be applicable to any . . . bicycle. . . .

TITLE 18. VEHICLES AND TRAFFIC (cont'd)
CHAPTER 22. MOVING VIOLATIONS
CHAPTER 24. STOPPING, STANDING, PARKING, AND OTHER NON-MOVING VIOLATIONS
CHAPTER 26. CIVIL FINES FOR MOVING AND NON MOVING INFRACTIONS

18 DCMR § 2202. Overtaking and passing

(2202.9) On any street where official traffic control devices have been erected giving notice that bicycles are entitled to the use of the full right-hand lane then available for moving traffic, the driver of a motor vehicle shall not drive within that right hand lane while overtaking or passing a bicycle being driven in that lane, and after overtaking or passing, shall not drive into that right-hand lane until safely clear of the overtaken bicycle.

(2202.10) A person driving a motor vehicle shall exercise due care by leaving a safe distance, but in no case less than 3 feet, when overtaking and passing a bicycle.

18 DCMR § 2204. Turning requirements and restrictions

(2204.10) No vehicle shall make a U-turn so as to proceed in the opposite direction across a bicycle lane.

18 DCMR § 2400. Proper parking: General requirements and prohibitions

(2400.8) A person may park a . . . motorized bicycle in a direction other than parallel with the edge of the roadway, including perpendicular with the curb, if the . . . motorized bicycle does not obstruct the flow of traffic.

18 DCMR § 2405. Stopping, standing, or parking prohibited: No sign required

(2405.1) No person shall stop, stand, or park a motor vehicle or trailer in any of the following places, except when necessary to avoid conflict with other traffic, in compliance with law, or at the direction of a police officer or traffic control device:

(g) In a bicycle lane[34]

18 DCMR § 2411. Residential permit parking

(2411.13) While a [motorized bicycle] for which a residential parking permit has been issued is parked in the residential permit parking zone . . . the permit shall be affixed to a

---

[34] A violation of this provision is punishable by a civil fine of $65. 18 DCMR § 2600.1.

mounting tab which shall be bolted to either corner of the identification tag. Expired permits shall not be left visible on a vehicle after affixing a new permit.

18 DCMR § 2602. Bicycle infractions

(2602.1) The following civil infractions and their respective fines set forth in this section refer to bicycles and the operation of bicycles. The fine for any bicycle violation not listed in this section is twenty-five dollars ($25.00).

- Carrying objects which prevent operator from keeping one hand on the handle bars (§ 1201.6) $ 25.00
- Excessive number of riders (§ 1201.5) $ 25.00
- Furnishing false information (§ 1202.8) $ 25.00
- Hazardous driving (§ 1201.2) $ 25.00
- Hitching on vehicle (§ 1202.16) $ 25.00
- Impeding or obstructing traffic (§ 1201.3) $ 25.00
- Improper equipment (§ 1204) $ 25.00
- Improper securing of bicycle (§ 1209) $ 25.00
- Mounting race violation (§ 1206) $ 25.00
- Not riding on seat (§ 1201.4) $ 25.00
- Riding on sidewalk where not permitted (§ 1201.9) $ 25.00
- Riding abreast, obstructing traffic (§ 1201.7) $ 25.00
- Right-of-way, failure to yield (§ 1201, 10ff) $ 25.00
- Sounding of warning device (§ 1201.14; 1204.7) $ 25.00

- Speed, excessive (§ 1201.8) $ 25.00
- Traffic control, disobeying (§ 1201.15) $ 25.00

TITLE 18. VEHICLES AND TRAFFIC (cont'd)
CHAPTER 40. TRAFFIC SIGNS AND RESTRICTIONS AT SPECIFIC LOCATIONS[35]

18 DCMR § 4005. Restricted lanes

(4005.1) The traffic lane closest to the right hand curb on the streets listed in this subsection shall be designated a Restricted Lane and reserved for the use of [specified vehicles including] bicycles [and] motorized bikes . . . during the hours and on the days indicated.

(4005.2) The traffic lanes designated as High Occupancy Vehicle lanes on the streets listed under this subsection shall be reserved during the hours and days stated for each location for the use of [specified vehicles including] bicycles [and] motorized bikes. . . .

18 DCMR § 4023. Parking meter zones

(4023.5) . . . No person shall park any vehicle other than a motorcycle, motor-driven cycle, motor scooter, or motorized bicycle during the days and hours specified that the location is designated as a motorcycle parking meter zone.

[35] Note: The current version of the Regulations does not list specific locations for any of the provisions included here.

18 DCMR § 4028. Bicycle racks

(4028.1) Bicycle racks shall be established on the sidewalks or public parking areas at the locations listed in this section.

18 DCMR § 4029. Bicycle use of sidewalk areas

(4029.1) The riding of bicycles is prohibited on sidewalks within the Central Business District, as defined in this title, except on the streets listed in this subsection.

(4029.2) The riding of bicycles on sidewalks is permitted outside of the Central Business District, except on those streets listed in this subsection.

18 DCMR § 4033. Bicycle lanes

(4033.1) The lane(s) as indicated on the following streets shall be reserved for the use of bicycles and motorized bicycles; the operation of all other vehicles shall be prohibited within this lane.

18 DCMR § 413. Application for registration

(413.6) Only one (1) identification tag shall be issued for a motorized bicycle. . . .

18 DCMR § 601. Inspection requirements

(601.4) Except as provided in § 601.5, vehicles registered in the District of Columbia shall be inspected periodically for safe operating condition, exhaust emissions, and compliance with this Title as follows:

(f) Motorized bicycle, except those rented to or offered to be rented to the public: every two (2) years;

(g) Motorized bicycle rented to or offered to be rented to the public: annually. . . .

(601.8) The fees for inspections shall be as follows:

(b) Motorized bicycle: $35

18 DCMR § 607. Placement of inspection stickers on vehicles

(607.3) "Approved" stickers, "rejection" stickers, "condemned" stickers, temporary inspection stickers and temporary registration certificates for . . . motorized bicycles . . . shall be affixed to the identification tag. Mounting tabs shall be bolted to either corner of the identification tag.

18 DCMR § 1110. Penalties for violations

(1110.6) Any person found violating subsection 1200.8 of Chapter 12 (which prohibits tampering with a bicycle locked or placed in a rack, or otherwise secured), shall be punished by a fine of not more than three hundred dollars ($300.00) or imprisonment not to exceed ten (10) days.

18 DCMR § 9901. Definitions

Bicycle - a device which is propelled solely by human power; which is designed to be ridden by one (1) or more persons; which has a saddle or seat for each person that the device is designed and equipped to carry; which has a tandem arrangement of two (2) wheels (or is a device generally recognized as a bicycle though equipped with two front or rear wheels); and which has either one wheel at least twenty inches (20 in.) in diameter or is designed to be ridden on a roadway. This shall not include any device equipped with a motor or engine capable of propelling such device either exclusively or in combination with human power, whether or not such motor or engine is in actual operation. (D.C. Law 1-110).

Driver or Operator - a person who drives or is in actual physical control of a vehicle or bicycle.

Motorized Bicycle - any motor vehicle having either a tandem arrangement of two wheels equipped with tires which are sixteen inches (16 in.) or more in diameter or a tricyclic arrangement of three (3) wheels equipped with tires which are sixteen inches (16 in.) or more in diameter, having a seat or saddle for the use of the operator, having an automatic transmission, and having a motor or engine which produces not more than one and one-half (1.5) brake horsepower (S.A.E. rating), has a piston displacement of not more than fifty cubic centimeters (50 cc), and is capable of moving the vehicle at a maximum speed of not more than thirty-five miles per hour (35 mph) on level ground when propelled exclusively by such motor or engine. (D.C. Law 1-110 & D.C. Law 3-125)

Mountable (bicycle) Rack - any device designed for the use of transporting one or more bicycles by means of a motor vehicle. (Reg. No. 71-26)

Operate (a bicycle) - to ride, walk with, park, stand, or be in possession of a bicycle on public space within the District. (C.O. 71-26)

Owner - any of the following: (D.C. Law 2-104)

(a) Any person, corporation, firm, agency, association, organization, or federal, state, or local government agency or other authority or other entity having the property of or title to a vehicle or bicycle used or operated in the District;

(c) Any person, corporation, firm, agency, association, organization, Federal, State or local government agency or authority or other entity in the business of renting or leasing vehicles or bicycles to be used or operated in the District; and

(d) Any person who is a parent or guardian of a child less than eighteen years of age who possesses a bicycle shall be the "owner."

Pedicab – a bicycle with a single frame that connects two (2) rear wheels and one (1) front wheel that is designed to be ridden by one (1) or more persons, that transports, or is capable of transporting, passengers on seats attached to the bicycle, and that is used for transporting passengers for hire.

Rack - any device designed for the temporary storage of one or more bicycles. (Reg. No. 71-26)

Restricted Lanes - traffic lanes where use is restricted according to class of vehicle occupancy or type of vehicle, for example: buses; carpools; taxicabs; motorcycles; bicycles; motorized bicycles; high occupancy vehicles (HOV); and vehicles transporting handicapped persons. (35. DCR 2204)

Serial Number (bicycle) - a number stamped on a bicycle frame in accordance with this title, which is recorded for purposes of verifying bicycle ownership. (Reg. No. 71-26)

Sidewalk Bicycle - a device which would be included within the definition of "bicycle" as set forth in this section, except for the fact that such device either has two (2) or more wheels, all of which are less than twenty inches (20. in.) in diameter, or is not designed to be ridden on a roadway. (Reg. No. 71-26)

TITLE 11. ZONING
MISC. REGULATIONS

11 DCMR § 199. Definitions

(199.1) When used in this title, the following terms and phrases shall have the meanings ascribed:

Parking space, bicycle - a space for the temporary storage of a bicycle in the form of a rack, locker, or storage area of appropriate design and dimension, used exclusively for the storage of a bicycle. (31 DCR 6585)

Recreational building or use - any establishment providing facilities for recreation; including . . . bicycling . . . and activities incidental [thereto]. . . . (21 DCR 1030)

11 DCMR § 2119. Bicycle parking spaces

(2119.1) Bicycle parking spaces shall be provided for office and retail and service uses. . . .[36]

(2119.2) The number of bicycle parking spaces provided shall be at least equal to five percent (5%) of the number of

[36] A violation of this provision is a Class 3 infraction. 16 DCMR § 3312.3(i).

automobile parking spaces required under § 2101.1.[37]

(2119.3) Bicycle facilities shall have convenient access from the building or structure and street or other bicycle right-of-way and shall be clean, secure, well-lit, and located within a building or structure, either on the ground floor, basement, or first cellar level.

(2119.4) All bicycle parking spaces required under § 2119.1 shall be a minimum of two feet (2 ft.) in width and six feet (6 ft.) in length.

(2119.5) An aisle five feet (5 ft.) in width shall be provided between rows of bicycle parking spaces and the perimeter of the area devoted to bicycle parking.

(2119.6) If a room or common locker not divided into individual spaces is used to meet these requirements, twelve square feet (12 ft.2) of floor area shall be considered the equivalent of one (1) bicycle parking space. Where manufactured metal lockers or racks are provided, each locker or stall devoted to bicycle parking shall be counted as one bicycle parking space.

(2119.7) [DELETED]

(2119.8) Signs shall be posted stating where bicycle parking spaces are located in each building or structure where bicycle parking spaces are required. The signs shall be located in a prominent place at each entrance to the building or structure. The sign shall have a white background, with black lettering

---

[37] A violation of this provision is a Class 3 infraction. 16 DCMR § 3312.3(m).

that is no less than two inches (2 in.) in height.[38]

(2119.9) For a building or structure existing on March 1, 1985, one percent (1%) of the amount of required parking spaces may be converted to bicycle parking spaces of appropriate size.

(2119.10) For a marina or yacht club within the W-0 District, one suitably designed and sited bicycle rack parking space shall be provided for each ten (10) berths or mooring spaces, in a location that is secure and convenient to the principal structure.

(2119.11) For a boathouse within the W-0 District, one suitably designed and sited bicycle rack parking space shall be provided for each 2,000 gross square feet of gross building area, in a location that is secure and convenient to the principal structure.

11 DCMR § 2910. Bicycle parking

(2910.1) Bicycle parking spaces shall be provided at a minimum as follows:

[38] A violation of this provision is a Class 4 infraction. 16 DCMR § 3312.4(t).

TYPE OF USE	INDOOR SPACES	OUTDOOR SPACES
Residential	1 for every 3 units	1 for every 20 units with a minimum of 2
Non-residential	1 for every 10,000 square feet of gross floor area, with a minimum of 2	1 for every 40,000 square feet of gross floor area, with a minimum of 2
Retail/service	1 for every 10,000 square feet of gross floor area, with a minimum of 2	1 for every 5,000 square feet of gross floor area, with a minimum of 2

(2910.2) All bicycle parking spaces shall be well lit and provide convenient access to the uses they are intended to serve.

(2910.3) Outdoor spaces may be provided in public space subject to the approval of the District Department of Transportation (DDOT).

(2910.4) All required bicycle parking spaces shall be a minimum of two feet (2 ft.) in width and six feet (6 ft.) in length.

(2910.5) An aisle five feet (5 ft.) in width shall be provided between rows of bicycle parking spaces and the perimeter of the area devoted to bicycle parking.

(2910.6) If a room or common locker not divided into individual spaces is used to meet these requirements, twelve square feet (12 sq. ft.) of floor area shall be considered the equivalent of one (1) bicycle parking space. Where manufactured metal lockers or racks are provided, each locker or stall devoted to bicycle parking shall be counted as one (1) bicycle parking space.

(2910.7) Signs shall be posted stating where bicycle parking spaces are located in each building or structure where bicycle parking spaces are required. The signs shall be located in a prominent place at each entrance to the building or structure. The sign shall have a white background with black lettering that is no less than two inches (2 in.) in height.

11 DCMR § 3311. Bicycle parking

(3311.1) The bicycle parking standards of this chapter apply to all newly constructed buildings.

Bicycle parking spaces shall be provided in accordance with § 2119 of this title.

10-A DCMR § 409. Bicycle access, facilities, and safety [Planning and Development / Comprehensive Plan / Transportation Element]

(409.1) Bicycling has long been a part of the transportation mix in the District. In the late 19th and early 20th centuries, bicyclists, pedestrians, buggies, and streetcars all shared District streets. The District's interest in bicycling as an alternative to motorized transportation grew in the 1970s in response to the energy crisis and the first District Bicycle Plan was adopted in 1976.

(409.2) The use of bicycles for transportation and recreation is increasing within the District. Between 1990 and 2000, bicycle commuting grew by 55 percent, from a 0.75 percent share to a 1.16 percent share of all District-based work trips. Continued increases in bicycling as a percent of work trips is desired.

(409.3) Currently, the District has 17 miles of bike lanes, 50 miles of bike paths, and 64 miles of bicycle routes. The city is also working to improve bicycle connections through parks and green spaces. Map 4.3 shows the city's bicycle trail network.[39]

(409.4) While existing conditions provide a firm foundation for bicycling, many parts of the city are not as bicycle-friendly as they should be. Many parts of the city have no bicycle facilities at all and many workplaces and other destinations have no facilities for storing or locking bicycles.

(409.5) Safety is another big concern. On average there are 270 bicycle crashes in the city each year. Between 1992 and 2001, close to one-third of all fatalities from motor vehicle crashes in the District were pedestrians or bicyclists as compared to about 20 percent nationally and 27 percent for large urban areas.

(409.6) [See footnote 7]

(409.7) In 2003, the District Department of Transportation estimated the Bicycle Level of Services (Bicycle LOS) along

[39] Map 4.3: Bicycle Routes and Trails, available at http://planning.dc.gov/planning/frames.asp?doc=/planning/lib/planning/2006_revised_comp_plan/4_transportation.pdf.

400 miles of major collector and arterial streets in the District. The Department of Transportation evaluated roadway lane and shoulder width, speed limit, pavement condition, and on-street parking data. The analysis found that about 70 percent of the study network received below average Bicycle LOS grades. The recently completed Bicycle Master Plan includes many recommendations to improve bicycle facilities and infrastructure and should be consulted for more detail.

The use of bicycles for transportation and recreation is increasing within the District. Between 1990 and 2000, bicycle commuting grew by 55 percent, from a 0.75 percent share to a 1.16 percent share of all District-based work trips.

Please refer to the Parks, Recreation and Open Space Element for additional policies and actions related to bicycle and pedestrian trails.

(409.8) Policy T-2.3.1: Better Integration of Bicycle and Pedestrian Planning -- Integrate bicycle and pedestrian planning and safety considerations more fully into the planning and design of District roads, transit facilities, public buildings, and parks.

(409.9) Policy T-2.3.2: Bicycle Network -- Provide and maintain a safe, direct, and comprehensive bicycle network connecting neighborhoods, employment locations, public facilities, transit stations, parks, and other key destinations. Eliminate system gaps to provide continuous bicycle facilities. Increase dedicated bike-use infrastructure, such as bike-sharing programs like Capital Bikeshare, and identify bike boulevards or bike-only rights of way.

(409.10) Policy T-2.3.3: Bicycle Safety -- Increase bicycle safety through traffic calming measures, provision of public bicycle parking, enforcement of regulations requiring private bicycle parking, and improving bicycle access where barriers to bicycle travel now exist.

(409.11) Action T-2.3.A: Bicycle Facilities -- Wherever feasible, require large new commercial and residential buildings to be designed with features such as secure bicycle parking and lockers, bike racks, shower facilities, and other amenities that accommodate bicycle users.

(409.12) Action T-2.3.B: Bicycle Master Plan -- Implement the recommendations of the Bicycle Master Plan to: Improve and expand the bike route system [and]:

a. [P]rovide functional and distinctive signs for the system;

b. Provide additional bike facilities on roadways;

c. Complete ongoing trail development and improvement projects to close gaps in the system;

d. Improve bridge access for bicyclists;

e. Provide bicycle parking in public space and encourage bicycle parking in private space;

f. Update the District laws, regulations and policy documents to address bicycle accommodation;

g. Review District projects to accommodate bicycles;

h. Educate motorists and bicyclists about safe operating behavior;

i. Enforce traffic laws related to bicycling;

j. Establish a Youth Bicycle and Pedestrian Safety Education Program;

k. Distribute the District Bicycle Map to a wide audience; and

l. Set standards for safe bicycle operation, especially where bikes and pedestrians share the same space.

(409.13) Action T-2.3.C: Performance Measures -- Develop, apply, and report on walking and bicycle transportation performance measures to identify strengths, deficiencies, and potential improvements and to support the development of new and innovative facilities and programs.

(409.14) Action T-2.3.D: Bicycle Sharing -- Support the expansion of bicycle sharing kiosks throughout the District to develop a complete bicycle-sharing network and encourage bicycling.

17 DCMR § 114. Standard of review for evaluating the criminal history of an applicant for licensure or candidate for suspension or revocation of a license

(114.7) The following licenses require evaluation under both subsections 114.2[40] and 114.5[41]:

(D) Commercial bicycle operator

24 DCMR § 1108. Standards for amenities and street furniture

(1108.13) Bike racks shall meet the following criteria:

(a) The bike rack shall be an inverted U type. The bike rack shall support the frame of the bike at two locations; allow at

---

[40] (114.2) No application for any license shall be denied and no licensee shall have his or her license suspended or revoked, for any license listed in subsection 114.7, by reason of the applicant or licensee having been convicted of one or more criminal offenses in the District of Columbia or another jurisdiction, or by reason of a finding of lack of "good moral character," when such finding is based upon the fact that the applicant or licensee has been convicted of one or more criminal offenses in any jurisdiction, unless the board with jurisdiction over the matter first shows that:
(a) There is a potential direct relationship between the nature of one or more of the criminal offenses and the specific license sought or held; or
(b) The issuance or retention of the license could involve an unreasonable risk to property, safety, or welfare of specific individuals or the general public.

[41] (114.5) In making a determination pursuant to subsection 114.2 . . . the board or commission shall consider the following factors:
(a) The specific duties and responsibilities necessarily related to the license;
(b) The bearing, if any, the criminal offense or offenses for which the person was convicted will have on his fitness or ability to perform one or more such duties or responsibilities under the license;
(c) The time that has elapsed since the occurrence of the criminal offense or offenses;
(d) The age of the person at the time of occurrence of the criminal offense or offenses;
(e) The nature and seriousness of the offense or offenses;
(f) Any information produced by the person, or produced on his behalf, concerning his or her rehabilitation and good conduct; and
(g) The legitimate interest of the public agency in protecting property, the safety, or welfare of specific individuals or the general public.

least one wheel along the frame to be locked to the rack; and allow cyclist the option of using either the popular U-lock or a cable with padlock;

(b) Bike racks shall be 2-3/8″ O.D. (outside diameter), galvanized, schedule 40 steel pipe, ASTM 53A, powder coated, gloss black, measuring thirty inches (30″) across and thirty six inches (36″) high above grade;

(c) Bike rack shall have minimum five feet (5′) clearance from other amenities and street furniture;

(d) Bike rack shall be placed parallel to the curb and three feet (3′) from the face of curb;

(e) Bike rack shall be placed within the typical twenty six feet (26′) distance from the end of the Metro Bus Stop Zone;

(f) Bike rack placement shall allow a minimum of ten feet (10′) of clearance for pedestrian flow; and

(g) Bike racks shall not be placed in an entrance or loading zone.

24 DCMR § 2001. Hazardous obstructions in public space

(2001.8) No proprietor of any . . . bicycle store . . . shall place or leave any hose or pipe on the curb, sidewalk, or parking at any time.

APPENDIX 3 THE STATE OF MARYLAND
MD. TRANSPORTATION CODE
TITLE 21. VEHICLE LAWS – RULES OF THE ROAD
SUBTITLE 12. OPERATION OF BICYCLES AND PLAY VEHICLES

Md. Code Ann., Transp. § 21-1201 (2013). Application of subtitle

(a) Authorizing minor or ward to violate subtitle prohibited-- The parent of any minor or the guardian of any ward may not authorize the minor or ward to violate any provision of this subtitle.

(b) Permitting minor or ward to violate subtitle prohibited -- The parent of any minor or the guardian of any ward may not knowingly permit the minor or ward to violate any provision of this subtitle.

(c) Operation of bicycles, EPAMDs, or motor scooters -- With the exceptions stated in this subtitle, the provisions of this subtitle that are applicable to bicycles apply whenever a bicycle, an EPAMD, or a motor scooter is operated on any highway or whenever a bicycle or an EPAMD is operated on any path set aside for the exclusive use of bicycles.

Md. Code Ann., Transp. § 21-1202 (2013). Bicycles and motor scooters required to obey traffic laws

Every person operating a bicycle or a motor scooter in a public bicycle area has all the rights granted to and is subject to all the duties required of the driver of a vehicle by this title, including the duties set forth in § 21-504[42] of this title, except:

(1) As otherwise provided in this subtitle; and

(2) For those provisions of this title that by their very nature cannot apply.

Md. Code Ann., Transp. § 21-1203 (2013). Operation of bicycles and motor scooters

(a) Operator seated astride permanent and regular seat -- The operator of a bicycle or a motor scooter may ride the bicycle or motor scooter only on or astride a permanent and regular seat securely attached to it.

(b) Bicycle passengers -- A bicycle may not carry any passenger unless it is designed for and equipped with a seat securely attached to it for each passenger.

Md. Code Ann., Transp. § 21-1204 (2013). Persons prohibited from clutching or attaching to vehicles

(b) Bicyclists and motor scooters -- A person riding on any

[42] Md. Code Ann., Transp. § 21-504 (2013). Duties of drivers relating to pedestrians
(a) Due care to avoid collisions -- Notwithstanding any other provision of this title, the driver of a vehicle shall exercise due care to avoid colliding with any pedestrian. Warning to pedestrian by sounding horn of vehicle
(b) Notwithstanding any other provision of this title, the driver of a vehicle shall, if necessary, warn any pedestrian by sounding the horn of the vehicle.
(c) Precautions for children or confused or incapacitated individuals -- Notwithstanding any other provision of this title, the driver of a vehicle shall exercise proper precaution on observing any child or any obviously confused or incapacitated individual.

bicycle or motor scooter may not attach it or himself to any vehicle on a roadway.

Md. Code Ann., Transp. § 21-1205 (2013). Operation of bicycles or motor scooters on roadways

(a) Riding near right side of roadway -- Each person operating a bicycle or a motor scooter at a speed less than the speed of traffic at the time and place and under the conditions then existing on a roadway shall ride as near to the right side of the roadway as practicable and safe, except when:

(1) Making or attempting to make a left turn;

(2) Operating on a one-way street;

(3) Passing a stopped or slower moving vehicle;

(4) Avoiding pedestrians or road hazards;

(5) The right lane is a right turn only lane; or

(6) Operating in a lane that is too narrow for a bicycle or motor scooter and another vehicle to travel safely side by side within the lane.

(b) Riding bicycles or motor scooters two abreast -- Each person operating a bicycle or a motor scooter on a roadway may ride two abreast only if the flow of traffic is unimpeded.

(c) Exercise of due care when passing vehicles -- Each person operating a bicycle or a motor scooter on a roadway shall exercise due care when passing a vehicle.

(d) Walking bicycle or motor scooter on right side of highway--

Each person operating a bicycle or a motor scooter on a roadway may walk the bicycle or motor scooter on the right side of a highway if there is no sidewalk.

Md. Code Ann., Transp. § 21-1205.1 (2013). Bicycle, motor scooter, and EPAMD restrictions

(a) In general -- Notwithstanding any other provision of this title, a person may not ride a bicycle or a motor scooter:

(1) On any roadway where the posted maximum speed limit is more than 50 miles an hour; or

(2) On any expressway, except on an adjacent bicycle path or way approved by the State Highway Administration, or on any other controlled access highway signed in accordance with § 21-313 of this title.

(b) Use of bike lane or shoulder paved to smooth surface required --

(1) Where there is not a bike lane paved to a smooth surface, a person operating a bicycle or a motor scooter may use the roadway or the shoulder.

(2) Where there is a bike lane paved to a smooth surface, a person operating a bicycle or a motor scooter shall use the bike lane and may not ride on the roadway, except in the following situations:

(i) When overtaking and passing another bicycle, motor scooter, pedestrian, or other vehicle within the bike lane if the overtaking and passing cannot be done safely within the bike lane;

(ii) When preparing for a left turn at an intersection or into an alley, private road, or driveway;

(iii) When reasonably necessary to leave the bike lane to avoid debris or other hazardous condition; or

(iv) When reasonably necessary to leave the bike lane because the bike lane is overlaid with a right turn lane, merge lane, or other marking that breaks the continuity of the bike lane.

(3) A person operating a bicycle or a motor scooter may not leave a bike lane until the movement can be made with reasonable safety and then only after giving an appropriate signal.

(4) The Department shall adopt regulations pertaining to this subsection, including a definition of "smooth surface".

Md. Code Ann., Transp. § 21-1206 (2013). Packages, bundles, or other articles transported by bicycle, EPAMD, or motor scooter

(a) Packages that prevent operator from keeping both hands on the handlebars -- A person may not operate a bicycle, an EPAMD, or a motor scooter while carrying any package, bundle, or other article that prevents the person from keeping both hands on the handlebars.

(b) Packages that interfere with view or balance of operator-- A person may not carry on a bicycle, an EPAMD, or a motor scooter any package, bundle, or other article that interferes with the view or balance of the operator.

(c) Tampering with bicycle prohibited -- A person may not

remove, ride on, or tamper with any part of a bicycle, an EPAMD, or a motor scooter without the permission of its owner.

Md. Code Ann., Transp. § 21-1207 (2013). Bicycle and motor scooter equipment requirements*

(a) Lamps and reflectors

(1) If a bicycle or a motor scooter is used on a highway at any time when, due to insufficient light or unfavorable atmospheric conditions, persons and vehicles on the highway are not clearly discernible at a distance of 1,000 feet, the bicycle or motor scooter shall be equipped:

(i) On the front, with a lamp that emits a white light visible from a distance of at least 500 feet to the front; and

(ii) On the rear, with a red reflector of a type approved by the Administration and visible from all distances from 600 feet to 100 feet to the rear when directly in front of lawful upper beams of head lamps on a motor vehicle.

(2) A bicycle or bicyclist may be equipped with a functioning lamp that acts as a reflector and emits a red light or a flashing amber light visible from a distance of 500 feet to the rear instead of or in addition to the red reflector required by paragraph (1) of this subsection.

(b) Bells or other devices -- Subject to subsection (c) of this section, a person may operate a bicycle or a motor scooter that is equipped with a bell or other device capable of giving a signal audible for a distance of at least 100 feet.

(c) Sirens or whistles -- A bicycle or motor scooter may not be equipped with nor may any person use on a bicycle any siren or whistle.

(d) Braking systems -- Every bicycle and motor scooter shall be equipped with a braking system capable of stopping from a speed of 10 miles per hour within 15 feet on dry, level, clean pavement.

Md. Code Ann., Transp. § 21-1207.1 (2013). Helmet use required for bicycle riders

(a) Application of section --

(1) The provisions of this section apply:

(i) At all times while a bicycle is being operated on any highway, bicycle way, or other property open to the public or used by the public for pedestrian or vehicular traffic; and

(ii) To a person under the age of 16 who is riding on a bicycle, including a person under the age of 16 who is a passenger on a bicycle:

1. In a restraining seat attached to the bicycle; or

2. In a trailer being towed by the bicycle.

(2) The provisions of this section do not apply to passengers in commercial bicycle rickshaws.

(b) Boardwalk at Ocean City -- This section does not apply in the town of Ocean City, Maryland, on the boardwalk between the Ocean City inlet and 27th Street, during the hours in which bicycles are permitted by local ordinance to be operated on the boardwalk.

(c) Helmet standards -- A person to whom this section applies may not operate or ride as a passenger on a bicycle unless the person is wearing a helmet that meets or exceeds the standards of the American National Standards Institute, the Snell Memorial Foundation, or the American Society for Testing and Materials for protective headgear for use in bicycling.

(d) Enforcement of section -- This section shall be enforced by the issuance of a warning that informs the offender of the requirements of this section and provides educational materials about bicycle helmet use.

Md. Code Ann., Transp. § 21-1208 (2013). Actions prohibited relating to bicycles, EPAMDs, or motor scooters

(a) Securing to fire hydrant, police or fire call box, or traffic control device -- A person may not secure a bicycle, an EPAMD, or a motor scooter to a fire hydrant, police or fire call box, or traffic control device.

(b) Securing to pole, meter, or device located within bus or taxi-loading zone -- A person may not secure a bicycle, an EPAMD, or a motor scooter to a pole, meter, or device located within a bus or taxi-loading zone.

(c) Securing to pole, meter, or device located within 25 feet of intersection -- A person may not secure a bicycle, an EPAMD, or a motor scooter to a pole, meter, or device located within 25 feet of any intersection.

(d) Securing to pole, meter, or device on which securing has been forbidden -- A person may not secure a bicycle, an

EPAMD, or a motor scooter to a pole, meter, or device on which notice has been posted by the appropriate authorities forbidding the securing of bicycles.

(e) Securing to place obstructing or impeding vehicular traffic or pedestrian movement -- A person may not secure a bicycle, an EPAMD, or a motor scooter to any place where the securing of a bicycle or a motor scooter would obstruct or impede vehicular traffic or pedestrian movement.

(f) Securing to parking meter -- A bicycle, an EPAMD, or a motor scooter may be secured to a parking meter, without payment of the usual fees, if it is entirely removed from the bed of the street normally used for vehicular parking.

Md. Code Ann., Transp. § 21-1209 (2013). Actions prohibited relating to bicyclists

(a) Drivers to exercise due care -- Notwithstanding any other provision of this title, the driver of a vehicle shall:

(1) Exercise due care to avoid colliding with any bicycle, EPAMD, or motor scooter being ridden by a person; and

(2) When overtaking a bicycle, an EPAMD, or a motor scooter, pass safely at a distance of not less than 3 feet, unless, at the time:

(i) The bicycle, EPAMD, or motor scooter rider fails to operate the vehicle in conformance with § 21-1205(a) of this subtitle ("Riding to right side of roadway") or § 21-1205.1(b) of this subtitle ("Roadway with bike lane or shoulder paved to smooth surface");

(ii) A passing clearance of less than 3 feet is caused solely by the bicycle, EPAMD, or motor scooter rider failing to maintain a steady course; or

(iii) The highway on which the vehicle is being driven is not wide enough to lawfully pass the bicycle, EPAMD, or motor scooter at a distance of at least 3 feet.

(b) Throwing objects at or in direction of person riding bicycle, EPAMD, or motor scooter -- A person may not throw any object at or in the direction of any person riding a bicycle, an EPAMD, or a motor scooter.

(c) Opening door with intent to strike or injure person riding bicycle, EPAMD, or motor scooter -- A person may not open the door of any motor vehicle with intent to strike, injure, or interfere with any person riding a bicycle, an EPAMD, or a motor scooter.

(d) Driver of vehicle to yield right of way -- Unless otherwise specified in this title, the driver of a vehicle shall yield the right-of-way to a person who is lawfully riding a bicycle, an EPAMD, or a motor scooter in a designated bike lane or shoulder if the driver of the vehicle is about to enter or cross the designated bike lane or shoulder.

Md. Code Ann., Transp. § 21-1210 (2013). Wearing headset while operating bicycle, EPAMD, or motor scooter prohibited

(a) Headsets covering both ears -- A person may not operate a bicycle, an EPAMD, or a motor scooter on any highway, or on any roadway, while the person is wearing any headset covering both ears.

(b) Earplugs in both ears -- A person may not operate a bicycle, an EPAMD, or a motor scooter on any highway, or on any roadway, while the person is wearing any earplugs in both ears.

(c) Application of section -- The provisions of this section do not apply to:

(1) Any person wearing personal hearing protectors in the form of custom earplugs or molds that are designed to attenuate injurious noise levels, if the custom plugs or molds are designed in such a manner as to not inhibit the wearer's ability to hear a siren or horn from an emergency vehicle or a horn from another vehicle;

(2) Any person wearing a prosthetic device used to aid the hard of hearing; or

(3) Any person operating a bicycle on a public bicycle pathway expressly authorized for the use of persons operating bicycles.

Md. Code Ann., Transp. § 21-1211 (2013). Approval required for motor vehicle and bicycle racing events

(a) Approval by Administration -- When the State Highway Administration or a local authority approves a motor vehicle or bicycle racing event on a highway or a highway bridge under its respective jurisdiction, motor vehicle or bicycle racing shall be lawful.

(b) Conditions for approval of racing event -- The State Highway Administration or a local authority may approve a motor vehicle or bicycle racing event only if:

(1) The racing event is held under conditions that:

(i) Provide reasonable safety for race participants, spectators, and other highway or highway bridge users; and

(ii) Prevent unreasonable interference with traffic flow that would seriously inconvenience other highway or highway bridge users;

(2) The sponsors of the racing event:

(i) Indemnify the State and local governments from any loss arising out of or relating to the racing event; and

(ii) Provide comprehensive liability insurance, in an amount to be determined by the State Highway Administration or local authority with jurisdiction over the highway on which the racing event is to be held, for the benefit of the State and local governments, spectators, and other highway or highway bridge users;

(3) The county or other local jurisdiction in which the racing event is held provides written authorization for the racing event; and

(4) The highway on which the racing event is held is closed, in a manner approved by the State Highway Administration or local authority with jurisdiction over the highway, with appropriate access measures in place.

(c) Compliance with other provisions of Maryland Vehicle Law -- If traffic control adequately assures the safety of participants, spectators, and other highway or highway bridge users, the State Highway Administration or a local authority may exempt participants in an approved motor vehicle or bicycle racing event from compliance with other provisions of the Maryland Vehicle Law that otherwise would be applicable to the participants in the motor vehicle or bicycle racing event.

Md. Code Ann., Transp. § 21-1212 (2013). Regulations published and made available to bicycle dealers and purchasers

The Administration shall publish copies or summaries of the regulations and laws of this State that regulate the operation of bicycles and make them available, on request and without cost, to every dealer engaged in the retail sale of bicycles in this State. These dealers shall provide a copy to each person who buys a bicycle.

MD. TRANSPORTATION CODE
TITLE 21. VEHICLE LAWS – RULES OF THE ROAD (cont'd)
MISC. PROVISIONS

Md. Code Ann., Transp. § 21-101 (2013). Definitions

(c) "Bicycle path" means any travelway designed and designated by signing or signing and marking for bicycle use, located within its own right-of-way or in a shared right-of-way, and physically separated from motor vehicle traffic by berm, shoulder, curb, or other similar device.

(d)(1) "Bicycle way" means:

(i) Any trail, path, part of a highway, surfaced or smooth shoulder, or sidewalk; or

(ii) Any other travelway specifically signed, marked, or otherwise designated for bicycle travel.

(2) "Bicycle way" includes:

(i) Bicycle path; and

(ii) Bike lane.

(e) "Bike lane" means any portion of a roadway or shoulder designated for single directional bicycle flow.

(i) "Crosswalk" means that part of a roadway that is:

(2) Within the prolongation or connection of the lateral lines of a bicycle way where a bicycle way and a roadway of any type meet or join, measured from the curbs or, in the absence of curbs, from the edges of the roadway . . .

(o) "Public bicycle area" means any highway, bicycle path, or other facility or area maintained by this State, a political subdivision of this State, or any of their agencies for the use of bicycles.

(v) "Shoulder" means that portion of a highway contiguous with the roadway for the accommodation of stopped vehicles, for emergency use, for use by bicycles and motor scooters, and for the lateral support of the base and surface courses of the roadway.

Md. Code Ann., Transp. § 21-202 (2013). Traffic circular lights and arrows; vehicle traffic and pedestrians

(e) Turning vehicles under (d) yield right of way to pedestrians[43] -- Vehicular traffic described under subsection (d) of this section shall yield the right-of-way to any pedestrian or bicycle lawfully within an adjacent crosswalk and to any other traffic lawfully using the intersection.

(k) Vehicle traffic in (i) and (j) yield right-of-way to pedestrians[44]-- In each instance, vehicular traffic described in subsections (i) and (j) of this section shall yield the right-of-way to any pedestrian or bicycle lawfully within an adjacent crosswalk and to any vehicle in the intersection or approaching on another roadway so closely as to constitute an immediate hazard.

Md. Code Ann., Transp. § 21-304 (2013). Vehicles allowed to overtake and pass to the right of another vehicle

(b) Passing another vehicle to right allowed if safe to do so -- The driver of a vehicle may overtake and pass another vehicle to the right only if it is safe to do so.

---

[43](d) Vehicular traffic facing a green arrow signal, whether shown alone or with another indication, cautiously may enter the intersection, but only to make the movement indicated by the arrow or to make another movement permitted by other indications shown at the same time.

[44] (i) Unless a sign prohibiting a turn is in place, vehicular traffic facing a steady red signal, after stopping as required by subsection (h) of this section, cautiously may enter the intersection and make:

(1) A right turn; or

(2) A left turn from a one-way street onto a one-way street.

(j) If a sign permitting any other turn is in place, vehicular traffic facing a steady red signal, after stopping as required by subsection (h) of this section, cautiously may enter the intersection and make the turn indicated by the sign.

(c) Driving off the roadway prohibited -- Except for an operator of a bicycle or motor scooter, a person may not make the movement described under subsection (b) of this section by driving off the roadway.

Md. Code Ann., Transp. § 21-313 (2013). Controlled access highway use restrictions

(a) Parades, low speed vehicles, funeral processions, bicycles, and motorcycles -- The State Highway Administration, by order, or any local authority, by ordinance, may prohibit the use of any controlled access highway in its jurisdiction by parades, low speed vehicles, funeral processions, bicycles, or other nonmotorized traffic or by any person operating a motorcycle.

Md. Code Ann., Transp. § 21-403 (2013). Rights of vehicles approaching intersection[45]

(a) Stop signs and yield signs -- Preferential right-of-way at an intersection may be indicated by stop signs or yield signs placed in accordance with the Maryland Vehicle Law.

(b) Vehicles approaching a through highway -- If the driver of a vehicle approaches a through highway, the driver shall:

(1) Stop at the entrance to the through highway; and

(2) Yield the right-of-way to any other vehicle approaching on the through highway.

---

[45] A bicycle is a "vehicle" for purposes of this provision. Gazvoda v. McCaslin, 36 Md. App. 604 (Md. Ct. Spec. App. 1977).

(c) Vehicles approaching stop sign at intersection -- If a stop sign is placed at the entrance to an intersecting highway, even if the intersecting highway is not part of a through highway, the driver of a vehicle approaching the intersecting highway shall:

(1) Stop in obedience to the stop sign; and

(2) Yield the right-of-way to any other vehicle approaching on the intersecting highway.

(d) Vehicles approaching yield sign at intersection -- If a "yield" sign facing the driver of a vehicle is placed on the approach to an intersection, the driver shall:

(1) Approach the intersection with caution;

(2) Yield the right-of-way to any other vehicle approaching on the other highway; and

(3) If necessary, stop in order to yield this right-of-way.

Md. Code Ann., Transp. § 21-604 (2013). Use of signals required to indicate turns, lane changes, and starts or stops of vehicles

(b) Turns made with reasonable safety -- A person may not turn a vehicle to enter a private road or driveway or otherwise turn a vehicle from a direct course or move it right or left on a roadway or from a shoulder or bikeway onto a roadway, unless the movement can be made with reasonable safety.

(d) Distance from which turn signal use required -- When required, a signal of intention to turn right or left shall be given continuously during at least the last 100 feet traveled by the vehicle before turning; except that a bicyclist may interrupt the turning signal to maintain control of the bicycle.

Md. Code Ann., Transp. § 21-606 (2013). Signals by hand

(c) Right turn signal -- A right turn signal is given by the hand and arm extended upward; except that a bicyclist may extend the right hand and arm horizontally to the right.

Md. Code Ann., Transp. § 21-1008 (2013). Accommodations and parking for bicycles

(a) Reasonable accommodations for bicycle access -- By fiscal year 2000, each public institution of higher education and State employment facility shall provide reasonable accommodations necessary for bicycle access, including parking for bicycles.

(b) Facility master plans to include bicycle and pedestrian transportation circulation -- When a public institution of higher education revises its facility master plan, the public institution of higher education shall address bicycle and pedestrian transportation circulation:

(1) Between the institution and the communities adjacent to the institution; and

(2) Within the campus of the institution.

(c) Promotion of walking and biking on campus -- The facility master plan shall include measures that the institution proposes to:

(1) Incorporate bikeways and pedestrian facilities on the campus; and

(2) Promote biking and walking on the campus.

Md. Code Ann., Transp. § 21-1103 (2013). Driving on sidewalk prohibited

(a) In general -- Except as provided in subsection (b), (c), or (d) of this section, a person may not drive any vehicle on a sidewalk or sidewalk area unless it is a permanent or authorized temporary driveway.

(b) Bicycle defined --

(1) For the purposes of this subsection, "bicycle" does not include "moped", as defined in § 11-134.1 of this article.

(2) Where allowed by local ordinance, a person may ride a bicycle, play vehicle, or unicycle on a sidewalk or sidewalk area.

(3) In a place where a person may ride a bicycle on a sidewalk or sidewalk area, a person may also ride a bicycle from the curb or edge of the roadway in or through a crosswalk to the opposite curb or edge of the roadway.

Md. Code Ann., Transp. § 21-1405 (2013). Pedestrians and bicycles prohibited from using vehicular crossing

(b) Bicycles -- Unless authorized by the Chairman of the Maryland Transportation Authority, bicycles may not use any Authority highway.

MD. TRANSPORTATION CODE
TITLE 8. HIGHWAYS

Md. Code Ann., Transp. § 8-204 (2013). Authority and responsibilities of [State Highway] Administration

(c) Duties relating to State highway system and bicycle and pedestrian priority areas

(1) The Administration shall:

(i) Determine and may change from time to time the location, construction, geometrics, design, and maintenance of the State highway system; and

(ii) 1. If the Administration and a local government designate an area as a bicycle and pedestrian priority area, implement a plan developed in cooperation with the local government to increase safety and access for bicycle or pedestrian traffic.

2. If there is no State highway within the limits of the bicycle and pedestrian priority area, the plan shall be developed by the local government.

(2) A plan for traffic management in a bicycle and pedestrian priority area shall provide for:

(i) Appropriate changes to the location, construction, geometrics, design, and maintenance of the State highway system to increase safety and access for bicycle or pedestrian traffic in the bicycle and pedestrian priority area; and

(ii) The appropriate use of traffic control devices including pedestrian control signals, traffic signals, stop signs, and speed bumps.

Md. Code Ann., Transp. § 8-409 (2013). Bicycle trails, footpaths, bridle paths, or horse trails

(a) Policy of State -- It is the policy of this State that bicycle trails are important and their construction is encouraged wherever feasible.

(b) User revenues to establish and maintain paths and trails-- To establish and maintain footpaths, bridle paths or horse trails, and bicycle trails:

(1) Baltimore City, any county, or any municipality that receives highway user revenues may spend a reasonable part of its net share for these purposes; and

(2) The Administration, Baltimore City, any county, or any municipality that receives highway user revenues may credit a part of them to a financial reserve or a special fund to be used within 10 years for these purposes.

(c) Restrictions on use of revenues -- Highway user revenues may not be used for footpaths, bridle paths or horse trails, or bicycle trails if:

(1) Their establishment would be contrary to public safety;

(2) Their cost would be too great considering their need or probable use; or

(3) The sparseness of population, the existence of other available ways, or other factors show that there is no need for them.

(d) [Technical assistance and advice] . . .

(e) Use of footpaths and bicycle trails -- Unless the Administration or local government specifically approves other uses, as provided in subsection (g) of this section, footpaths and bicycle trails may be used only by pedestrians, nonmotorized vehicles, and electric personal assistive mobility devices as defined in § 21-101(j) of this article.

(g) Specific approval of use by Administration or local government -- If the Administration or local government specifically approves the use of footpaths and bicycle trails by other than pedestrians and nonmotorized vehicles, . . . the Administration or local government shall post signs on the paths or trails indicating the uses specifically approved.

(h) Mopeds -- A person may not operate a moped on a footpath, bicycle trail, bridle path, or horse trail unless the path or trail is posted with signs in accordance with subsection (g) of this section specifically approving the use of mopeds.

(i) Sports cycles, trail bikes, and minibikes -- Notwithstanding the provisions of this subsection, the use of footpaths and bicycle trails shall be denied to sports cycles, trail bikes, and minibikes.

Md. Code Ann., Transp. § 8-601.1 (2013). Protection of existing bicycle routes

(a) The Administration may not construct any project that will result in the severance or destruction of an existing major route for bicycle transportation traffic, unless the project provides for construction of a reasonable alternative route or such a route already exists.

MD. TRANSPORTATION CODE (cont'd)
TITLE 2. DEPARTMENT OF TRANSPORTATION

Md. Code Ann., Transp. § 2-602 (2013). Legislative findings and declarations

The General Assembly finds that it is in the public interest for the State to include enhanced transportation facilities for pedestrians and bicycle riders as an essential component of the State's transportation system, and declares that it is the policy of the State that:

(1) Access to and use of transportation facilities by pedestrians and bicycle riders shall be considered and best engineering practices regarding the needs of bicycle riders and pedestrians shall be employed in all phases of transportation planning, including highway design, construction, reconstruction, and repair as well as expansion and improvement of other transportation facilities;

(2) The modal administrations in the Department shall ensure that the State maintains an integrated transportation system by working cooperatively to remove barriers, including restrictions on bicycle access to mass transit, that impede the free movement of individuals from one mode of transportation to another;

(3) As to any new transportation project or improvement to an existing transportation facility, the Department shall work to ensure that transportation options for pedestrians and bicycle riders will be enhanced and that pedestrian and bicycle access to transportation facilities will not be negatively impacted by the project or improvement; and

(4) In developing the annual Consolidated Transportation Program, the Department shall:

(i) Ensure that there is an appropriate balance between funding for:

1. Projects that retrofit existing transportation projects with facilities for pedestrians and bicycle riders; and

2. New highway construction projects; and

(ii) In transit-oriented areas within priority funding areas, as defined in § 5-7B-02 of the State Finance and Procurement Article, place increased emphasis on projects that retrofit existing transportation projects with facilities for pedestrians and bicycle riders and increase accessibility for the greatest number of pedestrians and bicycle riders.

Md. Code Ann., Transp. § 2-603 (2013). Director of Bicycle and Pedestrian Access

(a) There is a Director of Bicycle and Pedestrian Access in the Office of the Secretary.

(b)(2) The Director shall be a person with experience in transportation planning with specialized knowledge in matters relating to bicycle and pedestrian access to transportation facilities.

Md. Code Ann., Transp. § 2-604 (2013). Statewide 20-Year Bicycle-Pedestrian Master Plan

(a) Contents of Plan -- The Director shall develop and coordinate policies and plans for the provision, preservation, improvement, and expansion of access to transportation facilities in the State for pedestrians and bicycle riders, including development of a Statewide 20-Year Bicycle-Pedestrian Master Plan that:

(3) Provides a model to guide political subdivisions of the State in enhancing bicycle and pedestrian access to transportation facilities;

(4) Proposes long-term strategies for improving the State's highways to ensure compliance with the most advanced safety standards for pedestrians and bicycle riders; and

(5) After consultation with political subdivisions in the State, identifies bicycle-pedestrian priority areas to facilitate the targeting of available funds to those areas of the State most in need.

(b) [Review and update of Plan] . . .

(c) Powers and duties of Director -- To carry out the purposes of this subtitle, the Director shall:

(1) Participate in the planning of new transportation facilities and improvements to existing transportation facilities;

(2) Advise the Secretary on matters concerning bicycle and pedestrian access and any other matter as requested by the Secretary;

(3) Initiate a program of systematic identification of and planning for projects related to bicycle and pedestrian transportation that qualify for funds under Federal Highway Administration guidelines;

(4) Monitor State transportation plans, proposals, facilities, and services to ensure maximum benefits for pedestrians and bicycle riders in the State; and

(5) Consult regularly with the Bicycle and Pedestrian Advisory Committee established under § 2-606 of this subtitle.

Md. Code Ann., Transp. § 2-606 (2013). Bicycle and Pedestrian Advisory Committee

(a) The Governor shall appoint a Bicycle and Pedestrian Advisory Committee to provide guidance to State agencies concerning:

(1) Funding of bicycle and pedestrian related programs;

(2) Public education and awareness of bicycling and pedestrian related activities;

(3) Public education and awareness of bicycling and pedestrian safety; and

(4) Any other issue directly related to bicycling and pedestrians.

MD. TRANSPORTATION CODE (cont'd)

MISC. PROVISIONS

Md. Code Ann., Transp. § 7-902 (2013). [Mass transit; railroads]

(f) Regulations to facilitate transportation of bicycles -- The Administration shall adopt regulations to facilitate the transportation of bicycles on board passenger railroad services.

Md. Code Ann., Transp. § 11-104 (2013). Bicycle

"Bicycle" means a vehicle that:

(1) Is designed to be operated by human power;

(2) Has two or three wheels, of which one is more than 14 inches in diameter; and

(3) Has a drive mechanism other than by pedals directly attached to a drive wheel.

Md. Code Ann., Transp. § 13-102 (2013). Exceptions to certificate of title requirements

A certificate of title is not required for:

(7) A bicycle, except for a moped . . .

Md. Code Ann., Transp. § 25-102 (2013). Powers of local authorities relating to highways

(a) The provisions of the Maryland Vehicle Law do not prevent a local authority, in the reasonable exercise of its police power, from exercising the following powers as to highways under its jurisdiction:

(8) Regulating the operation of bicycles, requiring them to be registered, and imposing a registration fee . . .

Md. Code Ann., Transp. § 25-102.2 (2013). Operation of motorized passenger scooters

(c) Bicycle ways -- The State Highway Administration may prohibit the operation of a motorized passenger scooter on a bicycle way under the jurisdiction of the State Highway

Administration if it determines that:

(1) An occupant of a motorized passenger scooter is placed at an unacceptable risk of injury on the bicycle way; or

(2) The operation of a motorized passenger scooter is a threat to the safety or mobility of others along the bicycle way.

Md. Code Ann., Bus. Reg. § 12-301 (2013). Record of transactions

(b) Each pawnbroker shall make a written record . . . of each business transaction that involves:

(3) buying the following items for the purpose of resale:

(xi) bicycles . . .

APPENDIX 3(A)
MONTGOMERY COUNTY CODE AND REGULATIONS

<u>Overview</u>

Section I. Montgomery County Code

Section II. Code of Montgomery County Regulations (COMCOR)

MONTGOMERY COUNTY CODE

CHAPTER 7. BICYCLES

§ 7-1. Definitions

In this Chapter:

(a) bicycle means a vehicle designed:

(1) to be propelled only by human power;

(2) to carry one or more persons; and

(3) with 2 wheels, one of which is at least 16 inches in diameter; and

(b) bicycle helmet means a protective helmet designed for bicycle riders that is approved by the Snell Memorial Foundation or the American National Standards Institute, or that the Director of Transportation determines meets an equivalent standard.

§ 7-2. Bicycle helmets

A person who is under age 18 must wear a bicycle helmet when riding or being carried on a bicycle, including a bicycle with training wheels, on a public street, right-of-way, or bicycle path in the County.

§ 7-3. Persons providing bicycles for hire

A person who provides bicycles for hire must:

(a) not rent a bicycle to a person unless every person who is under age 18 and will ride or be carried on the bicycle has a bicycle helmet; and

(b) register under this Chapter every bicycle provided for hire.

§ 7-4. Bicycle registration[46]

[46] Violations of this provision are punishable by a civil fine of $10 (for initial violations) or $20 (for repeat violations). COMCOR § 01.19.02.04.

(a) Any County resident who owns a bicycle used on a public street, right-of-way, or bicycle path in the County must:

(1) register the bicycle by:

(A) completing a form provided by the County Executive or designee; and

(B) paying a registration fee; and

(2) have a legible County registration decal on the bicycle; and

(3) remove the County registration decal when the bicycle is sold, transferred, or dismantled.

(b) Bicycle registration under this Section is not transferable.

(c) A person, other than the owner, must not remove a County registration decal from a bicycle.

(d) The County Executive may set bicycle registration fees by executive regulation under method (3).

§ 7-5. Enforcement

(a) Enforcement. The County Police Department must enforce the requirements of this Chapter. The Maryland-National Capital Park and Planning Commission Police may enforce the requirements of this Chapter on Maryland-National Capital Park and Planning Commission property.

(b) Penalty. Any violation of this Chapter is a class C violation.

(c) Waiver.

(1) The fine for a person's first violation of a bicycle helmet requirement of this Chapter must be waived if:

(A) the person charged:

(i) is a minor; and

(ii) produces proof that the person has obtained a bicycle helmet for the person's use; or

(B) the person charged:

(i) is the parent or guardian of a minor; and

(ii) produces proof that the person has obtained a bicycle helmet for use by that minor.

(2) The citation for a person's first violation of a bicycle registration requirement of this Chapter must be rescinded if the person charged produces proof within 15 days after the citation is issued that the bicycle has been registered.

(d) Impoundment.

(1) The County Police Department and the Maryland-National Capital Park and Planning Commission Police may impound any unregistered bicycle until the bicycle is properly registered. The Maryland-National Capital Park and Planning Commission Police dispose of unregistered bicycles under Commission regulations.

(2) The County police must give an impounding receipt to the owner or operator of the unregistered bicycle. If an unregistered bicycle is impounded, the County police must hold an unregistered bicycle until it is:

(A) registered;

(B) donated to a non-profit organization that is exempt from taxation under Section 501(c)(3) of the Internal Revenue Code in the discretion of the Chief Administrative Officer if reasonable attempts to locate the owner are unsuccessful; or

(C) disposed of in the manner provided for abandoned motor vehicles under Section 31-63.[47]

(3) The net proceeds received from the sale of impounded or abandoned bicycles by the County police must be deposited in the Police Relief and Retirement Fund.

§ 7-6. Parental responsibility

A parent or guardian of a minor must not knowingly allow that minor to violate this Chapter.

§ 7-7. Evidence of negligence

47 § 31-63. Sales of abandoned, etc., vehicles – procedures generally Whenever any motor vehicle or part thereof is in the custody of the department of police and whenever the owner or person entitled to the possession thereof cannot be located and fails to claim such motor vehicle or part thereof for a period of sixty (60) days after such motor vehicle, or part thereof, came into the custody of the division, the same may be disposed of by the county executive, at public sale, at some time and place which shall be convenient and accessible to the public, provided, that an advertisement of the time, place and terms of the sale, together with a full, detailed description of such motor vehicle, or part thereof, shall be inserted in at least one (1) newspaper of general circulation in the county, at least once each week for two (2) successive weeks prior to the sale; provided, further, that a notice by registered mail shall be sent at least ten (10) days prior to the sale to the owner and lien holder, if any, shown on the records of the commissioner of motor vehicles, or the person entitled to the possession of such motor vehicle or part thereof, if his address be known, or if it can be ascertained by the exercise of reasonable diligence. If such address cannot be ascertained then such notice shall not be required.

Failure of a person to use a bicycle helmet as required by this Chapter, or evidence that a parent or guardian of a minor knowingly allowed the minor to violate a bicycle helmet requirement of this Chapter, must not:

(a) be considered evidence of negligence;

(b) be considered evidence of contributory negligence;

(c) limit liability of a party or an insurer; or

(d) diminish recovery for damages arising out of the ownership, maintenance, or operation of a motor vehicle.

MONTGOMERY COUNTY CODE
CHAPTER 31. MOTOR VEHICLES AND TRAFFIC

§ 31-1. Definitions

For the purposes of this chapter, the following words and phrases shall have the meanings respectively ascribed to them in this article:

Bicycle: A vehicle that is designed to be operated by human power or with assistance of a motor that has a capacity of less than fifty (50) cubic centimeters piston displacement or rated less than one (1) brake horsepower, that has two (2) or three (3) wheels of which one is more than fourteen (14) inches in diameter, that have a rear drive and with wheel configuration as follows:

(a) Two (2) wheels in tandem.

(b) Three (3) wheels; single front wheel with two (2) rear wheels on a horizontal axis perpendicular to the longitudinal plane of the front wheel and spaced substantially equidistant from the front wheel center line.

Recreational vehicle: A duly licensed and registered vehicle, with or without motor power, which is solely intended for the leisure use of the operator and guests. For the purpose of this Chapter the following is a recreational vehicle:

(d) non-freight trailer, as defined by the State Motor Vehicle Administration, used to transport other leisure equipment such as a . . . bicycle.

§ 31-5. Driving over curbs, sidewalks or drainage structures

(b) Bicycles which are not motorized and special vehicles used by handicapped persons may be operated upon sidewalk areas and appurtenant drainage structures designed for pedestrian use except where, in the judgment of the county executive, it is necessary for the safety or control of vehicular and pedestrian traffic to prohibit riding of such vehicles. Whenever any person is riding upon a sidewalk, such person shall give an audible signal and yield the right-of-way to any pedestrian . . .

(c) The county executive shall provide for the erection of such traffic-control signs on sidewalk areas or bikeways as may be necessary to ensure the safety of bicyclists, pedestrians and operators of motor vehicles; provided that no sign shall be erected on state highways without the approval of the state highway administration.

§ 31-28. Acts and conduct prohibited [in public parking facilities]

It shall be unlawful for any person to enter upon a county-operated public parking facility and:

(1) Engage in any conduct, sport or activity which may jeopardize the safety or welfare of persons or property, including but not limited to riding any [device such as a] bicycle . . .

§ 31-68. Pedestrian and bicycle safety impact statements

(a) For each applicable capital project in the Capital Improvements Program, the Office of Management and Budget must include in or transmit with the CIP an analysis of:

(1) the effect of the project on pedestrian and bicyclist access and safety in the project and the surrounding area; and

(2) what capital or operating modifications, if any, will be required to promote and maximize safe pedestrian and bicyclist access to, and in the area of, the project.

(b) As used in this section, applicable capital project includes:

(1) any new or modified building, road, park, school, or other capital project which is:

(A) proposed for development on a single unified site; and

(B) identifiable as a separate facility; and

(2) any project that comprises individual subprojects or items if any individual subproject or element listed in the project description form submitted by OMB, if treated separately, would be covered by paragraph (1).

(c) The Council may require any other County department or agency to supplement the analysis submitted by the Office of Management and Budget.

(d) The Council may by resolution exempt a category of capital projects which by their nature do not require an analysis under this Section.

MONTGOMERY COUNTY CODE
CHAPTER 49. STREETS AND ROADS

I. Article 1. In General

§ 49-1. Compliance with standards; regulations; penalty for violations

(a) A . . . bikeway must not be constructed, reconstructed, repaired, graded, improved or maintained by any person unless the construction, reconstruction, repair, improvement, grading or maintenance fully complies with this Chapter and any regulations issued under it.

(c) Any violation of this Chapter or any regulation issued under it is a Class B violation, except when expressly provided otherwise.

§ 49-9. Removal of items that obstruct the vision of motorists on public highways or interfere with the use of public rights-of-way

(a) Notice to owner of property. If the Director of Transportation finds that any tree, bush, vine, undergrowth, or other obstruction, except a building or similar structure affixed to the ground, on private property poses a threat to public safety by . . . restricting the use by pedestrians or bicyclists of the public rights-of-way, the Director promptly must serve on the owner, agent, lessee or any other person supervising the property a written notice that:

(1) describes where the obstruction exists;

(2) describes how the obstruction impairs the vision of operators of vehicles, including bicycles, or impedes pedestrian or legal bicycle travel on the right-of- way;

(3) describes the steps necessary to correct such conditions; and

(4) directs the person receiving the notice to take corrective steps within a stated period of time.

II. Article 3. Road Design and Construction Code

§ 49-26. Definitions

In this Chapter, except where specified otherwise, the following words and phrases have the meanings indicated:

Bikeway: any area expressly intended for bicycle travel, including any:

(a) Shared use path: A paved path 8′ - 12′ wide designated for bicycles and pedestrians that is separated from motorized traffic by a curb, barrier, or landscape panel.

(b) Bike lane: A portion of a roadway designated by striping, signing, or pavement markings for the preferential or exclusive use of bicycles, and on which through-travel by motor vehicles is not allowed.

(c) Shared use roadway: A roadway open to both bicycle and motor vehicle travel and which is designated as a preferred route for bicycle use by warning or informational signs.

§ 49-29. Pedestrian walkways, bikeways and wheelchair traffic

(a) Bikeways and walkways must be constructed when any County road is constructed, reconstructed, or relocated, unless the County Council finds (for a road improvement authorized in a capital improvements program) or the Planning Board finds (for a road improvement made a condition of preliminary plan or site plan approval) that bikeways or walkways in that location would reduce public safety, would not be feasible, or would be disproportionate in cost to their probable use. All bikeways and walkways must conform to approved capital improvements programs and be consistent with area master plans and transportation plans adopted by the Planning Board.

(b) To promote the safety of bicycle and wheelchair travel throughout the County, the County Executive must establish, by regulation, standards and specifications to build and maintain ramps at curbed intersections and storm water gratings and other openings along roads and streets, in each case of a design and type that is not a hazard to bicycle and wheelchair traffic. These ramps, gratings, and openings must be built and maintained as part of each project under subsection (a).

IV. <u>Miscellaneous</u>

§ 49-81. Pedestrian, Bicycle, and Traffic Safety Advisory Committee

(a) Definition. In this Section "Committee" means the Pedestrian, Bicycle, and Traffic Safety Advisory Committee.

(b) Established. The County Executive must appoint, subject to confirmation by the County Council, a Pedestrian, Bicycle, and Traffic Safety Advisory Committee.

(e) Duties. The Committee must:

(1) advise the Executive and Council on the status of the implementation of the recommendations in the Pedestrian Safety Final Report, issued in 2002;

(2) advise the Executive and Council of priorities and needs for pedestrian and bicycle safety and access, and other pedestrian-related issues; and

(3) continue to gather information on pedestrian safety and other pedestrian-related issues and identify new issues that emerge.

MONTGOMERY COUNTY CODE
MISC. PROVISIONS

§ 29-35A. Bicycle parking fees

(a) A landlord, the governing body of a common ownership community, or the owner or operator of a non-residential property that rents parking spaces for motor vehicles and bicycles must not charge rent or any other fee for parking a bicycle that exceeds the following fraction of any rent or fee charged for parking a motor vehicle:

(1) one-sixth, for a secure, fully enclosed bicycle locker; or

(2) one-tenth, for any other bicycle parking space.

(b) This Section does not require a landlord, a governing body, the owner or operator of a non-residential property, or any other person to charge rent or fees for bicycle parking.

§ 52-58. Use of impact tax funds

Impact tax funds may be used for any:

(a) new road or widening of an existing road that adds highway or intersection capacity or improves . . . bicycle commuting, such as . . . bike lanes;

(f) bicycle locker that holds at least 8 bicycles;

(g) bikesharing station (including bicycles) approved by the Department of Transportation. . . .

§ 54A-2. Prohibited conduct [in transit facilities]

A passenger in a public passenger vehicle or a person in a rail transit station must not:

(14) Operate, carry, or park any bicycle, tricycle, unicycle, motorcycle, motorbike or similar vehicle, unless:

a. The person carries a valid permit from WMATA or the county to transport the vehicle; and

b. The person complies with all conditions of the permit. . . .

§ 54A-5. Bicycles, motorcycles and similar vehicles [in transit facilities]

A person must not attach a bicycle, tricycle, unicycle, moped, motorcycle, motorbike or similar vehicle to a fence, tree, railing or other structure not specifically intended for that purpose on or near a station. A person must not park a bicycle, tricycle, unicycle, moped, motorcycle, motorbike or similar vehicle in an area not specifically intended for that purpose.

CODE OF MONTGOMERY COUNTY REGULATIONS (COMCOR)
MISC. REGULATIONS

Standard No. 010.01. Introduction and Application[48]

5.2.1. User Accommodation

In addition to medians, buffer areas, and maintenance offsets, the cross-sections are developed to accommodate users of the roadway through provisions of the following facilities within the cross-sections.

Bicyclists

Bicycle lanes

Shoulders

Shared lanes

[48] This provision is excerpted from Appendix A (Urban and Rural Boundaries) of COMCOR Chapter 49 (Streets and Roads).

Shared use paths

5.2.3. Cross-Section Element Widths

G. Bike Lanes

Bike Lanes are provided on closed-section roads. The following dimensions are indicated for different situations.

6- to 6.5-foot bike lanes are generally suitable on higher speed roads and adjacent to parking

6-foot bike lanes (inclusive of the gutter pan) are also generally suitable on Urban and Suburban closed section Major Highways

5.5-foot bike lanes (inclusive of the gutter pan) are generally suitable when adjacent to the curb on all roadway types except for Major Highway

52.47.01.06. [Development impact tax] credits

2. Under Section 52-55(b) a property owner must receive a credit for constructing or contributing to an improvement of the type listed in Section 52-58 if the improvement reduces traffic demand or provides additional transportation capacity[, including:]

1. A new road or widening of an existing road that adds highway or intersection capacity or improves transit service or bicycle commuting, such as bus lanes or bike lanes;

6. A bicycle locker that holds at least 8 bicycles.

Bicycle locker must be a new locker not a replacement locker.

Bicycle locker must be located at a major activity center or commuter transfer location where the locker would be used as a means to remove trips from the roadway network.

APPENDIX 3(B)
PRINCE GEORGE'S COUNTY CODE OF ORDINANCES
SUBTITLE 26. VEHICLES AND TRAFFIC
DIVISION 12. BICYCLES AND PLAY VEHICLES

§ 26-150. Designation of sidewalks and trails

The County Executive shall have the authority to designate or establish sidewalks or trails in Prince George's County for the exclusive or combined use of bicycles, play vehicles, or pedestrians provided that such designation or establishment would not be contrary to public safety, that the cost would not be excessively disproportionate to the projected need or use thereof, or that there is not a demonstrated absence of the projected need due to sparsity of population or the existence of other available facilities or other factors which demonstrate an absence of any need for such facilities. All new County financed road construction and reconstruction projects shall include facilities for the combined or exclusive use of bicycles, play vehicles, and pedestrians, except when cost shall be disproportionate to the projected need or when such facilities would be inappropriate due to the nature of the project or of the neighborhood. The location of such facilities shall not be limited to road rights-of-way, nor shall they be limited to locations parallel to roads.

§ 26-151. Exclusive use

If projected bicycle traffic or the safety of the cyclists or pedestrians justify a separate facility, bicycle trails for the exclusive use of bicycles shall be established.

§ 26-152. Motorized vehicles prohibited

No person shall stop, park, stand, or drive any motorized vehicle on any sidewalk or trail established under this Division. Any person issued a citation for a violation of this Section shall be subject to a fine of Ten Dollars ($10.00) for each offense.

§ 26-153. Signs posted

The Director shall erect or cause to be erected, posted, and maintained signs or other suitable identification at regular intervals.

§ 26-154. Applicable laws

Any sidewalk or trail designated or established by the County Executive for use by bicycles shall be deemed to be a public bicycle area and every person operating a bicycle thereon shall be subject to the applicable provisions of the Laws of the State of Maryland.

§ 26-101. Definitions

(a) For the purposes of this Subtitle, the following words and phrases shall have the meanings respectively ascribed to them hereunder:

(1) Bicycle means a vehicle that is designed to be operated by human power or with assistance of a motor that has a capacity of less than 50 cubic centimeters piston displacement or rated

less than one brake horsepower, that has two or three wheels of which one is more than 14 inches in diameter, that have a rear drive, and with wheel configuration as follows:

(A) Two wheels — in tandem;

(B) Three wheels — single front wheel with two rear wheels on a horizontal axis perpendicular to the longitudinal plane of the front wheel and spaced equidistant from the front wheel centerline;

(C) For the purposes of this Subtitle, a two or three wheeled vehicle operated by human power and not defined as a bicycle herein shall be considered a "play vehicle."

(12) Operate a Bicycle means to propel a bicycle by human power or to walk or stand with or otherwise be in control of a bicycle incidental to its propulsion, but does not include the carrying or transporting of a bicycle, without any passenger or rider thereupon, in any vehicle or carton or by any other similar means.

(15) Public Bicycle Area means any highway, street, sidewalk, bicycle path, or other facility or area maintained by the State or designated, established, or maintained by the County pursuant to this Subtitle for the exclusive or nonexclusive use of bicycles.

§26-146. Acts and conduct prohibited [in public parking facilities]

(a) It shall be unlawful for any person to enter upon a public parking facility and:

(1) Engage in any conduct, sport, or activity which may

jeopardize the safety or welfare of persons or property including . . . riding any . . . bicycle. . . .

MISC. REGULATIONS (OTHER)

§ 20A-102. Prohibited conduct [in public passenger vehicles]

(a) It shall be unlawful for any passenger or occupant aboard a public passenger vehicle, whenever said vehicle is transporting passengers in regular route service within the corporate (designated) limits of Prince George's County, Maryland, or any person in a rail transit station located within the corporate (designated) limits of Prince George's County, Maryland, to:

(14) Park, operate, carry, wheel, or chain to any fence, tree, railing, or other structure not specifically designated for such use, bicycles, tricycles, unicycles, mopeds, motorbikes, or any such vehicle, unless said person has in his possession a valid, current permit issued by WMATA for the transporting of noncollapsible bicycles by rail transit and said person is complying with all terms and conditions of said permit. . . .

§ 24-124.01. Adequate public pedestrian and bikeway facilities required in County Centers and Corridors

(a) . . . Pedestrian and bikeway facilities should be designed to increase safety, reduce travel time and offer the most direct routes to destinations for persons of all abilities. . . .

(b)(2) The finding of adequate public bikeway facilities shall, at a minimum, include the following criteria:

(B) the presence of specially marked and striped bike lanes or paved shoulders in which bikers can safely travel without unnecessarily conflicting with pedestrians or motorized vehicles;

(C) the degree to which protected bicycle lanes, on-street vehicle parking, medians, or other physical buffers exist to make it safer or more inviting for bicyclists to traverse the area; and

(D) the availability of safe, accessible, and adequate bicycle parking at transit stops, commercial areas, employment centers, and other places where vehicle parking, visitors, and/or patrons are normally anticipated.

(j)(2) Bicycle and pedestrian ways (including but not limited to continuous sidewalks on both sides of all streets and appropriate on-road bicycle facilities in each direction of travel on roads other than local and high-speed roads) shall be provided in all new construction and reconstruction projects and all roadway capital improvement projects in Centers and Corridors unless bicyclists and pedestrians are prohibited by law from using the roadway, the cost of constructing the pedestrian or bikeway facilities substantially encumbers the public benefit of the proposed development project, or other topographic or environmental factors would effectively prohibit pedestrian or bicycle travel.

§ 27A-707. Bicycle parking

(a) Required Spaces.

(1) All new nonresidential development providing less than twenty (20) vehicle parking spaces shall provide four (4) bicycle parking spaces for each ten-thousand (10,000) square feet of nonresidential development. A minimum of four (4)

bicycle parking spaces shall be provided by all nonresidential development regardless of size.

(2) Nonresidential development providing more than twenty (20) but less than one hundred one (101) vehicle parking spaces shall be required to install a minimum of six (6) bicycle parking spaces. Six (6) additional bicycle parking spaces shall be required for every 100 additional vehicle parking spaces.

(3) All new residential development providing more than twenty (20) but less than one hundred one (101) vehicle parking spaces shall be required to install a minimum of ten (10) bicycle parking spaces. Ten (10) additional bicycle parking spaces shall be required for every 100 additional vehicle parking spaces.

(4) Single-family detached and single-family attached dwellings are exempt from this requirement.

(5) Wheel racks shall not be counted toward meeting the minimum bicycle parking requirements.

(b) Bicycle Parking Design Regulations.

(1) Bicycle parking spaces should be located at close to the building entrance as possible. At least four (4) of the required bicycle parking spaces serving nonresidential development shall be located within fifty (50) feet of the main entrance to the building.

(2) When located outdoors, bicycle parking spaces shall be installed in concrete footings with anchor bolts.

(3) Bicycle parking spaces shall be placed at least three (3) feet away from the associated structure to allow sufficient room

for parking a bicycle. Bicycle racks should be installed to allow for at least thirty (30) inches of spacing between each rack. Where serpentine rows of bicycle parking is provided, an aisle at least five (5) feet in width shall be provided between rows of bicycle parking spaces, and along the perimeter of the area devoted to bicycle parking.

(4) Covered bicycle parking spaces should be provided whenever possible. All bicycle parking areas serving residential development shall be in a covered location that is well-lit and placed to allow for increased observation by passers-by in keeping with best practices of CPTED [Crime Prevention Through Environmental Design].

APPENDIX 4
PREPARING FOR YOUR DEPOSITION
TIPS FOR WITNESSES

1. Tell the truth. Not just because it is the right thing to do, but also because it's the smart thing to do. You will also need to divorce what you have come to learn through the litigation or post-event processes from what you knew on the day you are being questioned about at the deposition.

2. Don't be too nervous, but don't be too relaxed. A little anxiety is to be expected and is probably a good sign that your adrenaline is flowing and keeping you alert. There is no need, however, to be overly nervous. You are simply answering questions concerning your knowledge and information about the matter in dispute. At the same time, do not get too relaxed. A deposition has the appearance of a normal conversation, but it is *not*. It is a formal procedure with potentially serious consequences.

3. Think before you speak. Make sure the questioner has finished the question and pause briefly before answering. This allows counsel to formulate objections and further allows you to reflect on what your answer will be. The transcript will not record that you waited one second or one hour before making your answer.

4. Answer the question. The examiner is entitled to an answer to the question asked and only to that question.

5. Do not volunteer. You are not there to educate the examiner. If the examiner appears totally confused about your business and its technical aspects, resist the urge to educate the examiner.

6. Do not answer a question you do not understand. It is up to the examiner to frame intelligible questions. If he or she cannot do so, do not offer to help. Do not help the examiner by saying "do you mean `x' or do you mean `y.'"? You will then be asked both questions.

7. Talk in complete sentences. Beware of questions with double negatives.

8. Do not guess. If you do not know or cannot recall something, say so. There is nothing wrong with a truthful statement that you do not know or do not remember. You may be asked if a statement or document refreshes your recollection. If it does, say so. If it does not, the answer remains that you do not remember. Do not underestimate the "powers" of defense counsel through subpoenas, interviews, and surveillance to corroborate or impeach your testimony.

9. Do not be put in a position contrary to your true recollection. If you are asked when something occurred and you remember that it occurred, for example, on January 15, state "on January 15." If you cannot recall the exact date, state the approximate date.

10. Do not be defensive. Answer the questions directly and forthrightly. Resist the temptation to explain or justify answers.

11. If you are finished with an answer and the answer is complete and truthful, remain quiet and do not expand upon it. Do not add to your answer because the examiner looks at you expectantly. If the examiner asks you if that is all you recollect, say yes if that is the case. Do not feel the need to fill silences.

12. Never characterize your own testimony. Do not use "in all candor," "honestly," "I am doing the best I can," or similar phrases.

13. Avoid adjectives and superlatives. "I never" or "I always" can have a way of coming back to haunt you. This is also known as the "Mark Furhman trap." The only exception to that rule is with time lapse estimates. If you do not know precisely how long something took to occur, do not guess but state "very short," "very long," etc.

14. Do not testify as to what other people know unless you are asked specifically for such a statement.

15. Numerous documents are typically marked as exhibits at deposition. Before testifying about a document, read it.

Do not make any comments whatsoever about the document except to answer a question.

16. If the requested information is in a document which is an exhibit, ask to see the document unless you are very certain of your answer.

17. If the information is in a document that is not an exhibit to the deposition, answer the question if you can recall the answer. Do not tip off the examiner as to the existence of documents he or she does not know about.

18. Do not let the examiner put words in your mouth. Do not accept the examiner's characterization of time, distances, personalities, events, and the like. Rephrase the question into a sentence of your own using your own words. Do not always assume that if it's written down that it is true, accurate, or demonstrates that your recollection is incorrect.

19. Pay particular attention to the introductory clauses preceding the guts of the question. Leading questions are often preceded by statements that are either half true or contain facts that you do not know to be true. Do not have the examiner put you in the position of adopting these half truths, unknown facts, or his or her "spin" on the facts. Be aware that if you adopt those characterizations, he or she will then base further questioning on them.

20. If you are interrupted, let the lawyer finish the interruption and then firmly but courteously state that you were interrupted and that you had not yet finished your answer to the previous question, and then answer that question.

21. If you are caught in an inconsistency, do not collapse. What will happen next will depend upon what questions are asked of you. State, if asked, your present recollection. State the reason for the inconsistency only if you are asked. Your counsel will be responsible for rehabilitation either when it is your counsel's turn to ask questions or at trial.

22. Do not expect to testify without the other side "scoring some points." If the other side appears to be asking some questions which call for answers that do not help your case, accept the fact that every lawsuit has two sides. Avoid the temptation to guess or expand on your answer where expansion is not called for or to be equivocal in your response.

23. Every witness makes mistakes at a deposition. Do not become upset if you find you have made one. If you realize you have made a mistake, correct it as soon as it is realized.

24. Never express anger or argue with the examiner. If a deposition becomes unpleasant, your counsel will deal with the situation. Do not allow the other attorney to learn how to "press your buttons," because it can come back to haunt you at trial. As difficult as it may be, try to keep the emotion, anger, and frustration out of your testimony.

25. Avoid any attempt at levity.

26. Avoid even the mildest obscenity and absolutely avoid any ethnic slurs or references that could be considered as derogatory.

27. There is no such thing as "off the record." If you have a conversation with anybody in the deposition room, be prepared for questions about the conversation.

28. If you are hit with a flash of insight or recollection while testifying that has not been previously discussed with your counsel, keep the matter to yourself, if possible, until you have had an opportunity to go over it with counsel.

29. Dress and act conservatively at the deposition. In this instance, first impressions are important impressions.

30. Keep your counsel informed. Please remember that it is easier to stay out of trouble than to stop trouble once it has begun. Please keep your counsel informed and please disclose to your counsel anything that may have any impact on the case. Please also remember that if this is a personal injury suit, your medical, employment, and insurance records (not just those related to the accident or incident) may be subject to subpoena. Those records can provide a great deal of ammunition to opposing counsel. Your counsel cannot minimize their impact if the facts and opinions that may be recorded in those records are unknown to your counsel. The contents of those records are properly the subject of questions at a deposition.

APPENDIX 5
BICYCLE SAFETY AND RELATED CYCLING RESOURCES

National, State, and Regional Groups:

Washington Area Bicyclist Association -- http://www.waba.org

League of American Bicyclists -- http://www.bikeleague.org

Alliance for Biking and Walking -- http://www.peoplepoweredmovement.org

America Bikes -- http://www.americabikes.org

Association of Pedestrian and Bicycle Professionals -- http://www.apbp.org

Bicycle Helmet Safety Institute -- http://www.helmets.org

Bike Collective Network -- http://www.bikecollectives.org

Bike Maryland -- http://bikemd.org

Bike Pure -- http://bikepure.org

Bike Virginia -- http://bikewalkvirginia.org

Bikes Belong -- http://www.bikesbelong.org

Bikes for the World -- http://www.bikesfortheworld.org

Cadence Cycling Foundation -- http://www.cadencefoundation.org

Capital Bikeshare -- http://www.capitalbikeshare.com

Cycling Savvy -- http://cyclingsavvy.org

National Center for Bicycling & Walking -- http://www.bikewalk.org

National Center for Safe Routes to School -- http://www.saferoutesinfo.org

National Complete Streets Coalition -- http://www.smartgrowthamerica.org/complete-streets

National Transportation Alternatives Clearinghouse -- http://www.ta-clearinghouse.info

NoVa Smart Cycling -- http://novasmartcycling.blogspot.com

One Street -- http://www.onestreet.org

Pedestrian and Bicycle Information Center -- http://www.bicyclinginfo.org

People for Bikes -- http://www.peopleforbikes.org

Planet Bike -- http://planetbike.com

Potomac Pedalers -- http://www.potomacpedalers.org

ProBicycle -- http://probicycle.com

SRAM Cycling Fund -- http://www.sramcyclingfund.com

USA Cycling -- http://usacycling.org

United States Deaf Cycling Association -- http://usdeafcycling.org

Virginia Bicycling Federation -- http://www.vabike.org

Walk/Bike to School -- http://www.walkbiketoschool.org

WashCycle (blog) -- http://washcycle.typepad.com

World Bicycle Relief -- http://worldbicyclerelief.org

Yield to Life -- http://www.yieldtolife.org

Local Groups:

Baltimore Bicycle Advocacy Organization -- http://bikemore.net

Baltimore Bicycling Club -- http://baltobikeclub.org

Bicycling Advocates of Howard County -- http://bikehoco.org

Bike Arlington -- http://www.bikearlington.com

Bike Loudon -- http://www.bikeloudoun.org

College Park Area Bicycle Coalition -- http://cpabc.org

Fairfax Advocates for Better Bicycling -- http://www.fabb-bikes.org

Local Bicycle Repair Cooperatives

The Bike House (DC) -- http://www.thebikehouse.coop

Phoenix Bikes (Arlington) -- http://www.phoenixbikes.org

VéloCity Bicycle Cooperative (Alexandria) --
http://velocitycoop.org

Mountain/Trail Biking

Adventure Cycling Association --
http://www.adventurecycling.org

Fountainhead Project --
http://www.fountainheadproject.org

International Mountain Biking Association --
http://www.imba.com

International Police Mountain Biking Association --
http://www.ipmba.org

Mid-Atlantic Off-Road Enthusiasts (MORE) --
http://www.more-mtb.org

ABOUT THE AUTHOR

BRUCE DEMING is a competitive cyclist and trial attorney with over thirty years of litigation experience. In 2005, his four-man team completed the famous Race Across America (RAAM) in 7 days, 14 hours.

In recent years, he has earned numerous podium finishes in long distance mountain bike races throughout the U.S., including 9, 12 and 24 hour events. In 2012, he won his solo division age group in the 24 Hours of Great Glen mountain bike race at Mt. Washington, NH.

Mr. Deming is also an accomplished mountaineer, having summited peaks in the Alaska Range (Denali), the Andes, the Alps, and the Himalayas, including 22,493′ Ama Dablam in the Khumbu Region of Nepal.

He resides in Arlington, Virginia with his wife Belle Clay and his daughter, Celia Clay.

WA